THE PELICAN SHAKESPEARE
GENERAL EDITORS

STEPHEN ORGEL
A. R. BRAUNMULLER

The Winter's Tale

Ellen Terry as Hermione, 1906

William Shakespeare

———

The Winter's Tale

EDITED BY FRANCES E. DOLAN

PENGUIN BOOKS

PENGUIN BOOKS
Published by the Penguin Group
Penguin Putnam Inc., 375 Hudson Street,
New York, New York 10014, U.S.A.
Penguin Books Ltd, 80 Strand, London WC2R 0RL, England
Penguin Books Australia Ltd, 250 Camberwell Road,
Camberwell, Victoria 3124, Australia
Penguin Books Canada Ltd, 10 Alcorn Avenue,
Toronto, Ontario, Canada M4V 3B2
Penguin Books India (P) Ltd, 11 Community Centre,
Panchsheel Park, New Delhi – 110 017, India
Penguin Books (N.Z.) Ltd, Cnr Rosedale and Airborne Roads,
Albany, Auckland, New Zealand
Penguin Books (South Africa) (Pty) Ltd, 24 Sturdee Avenue,
Rosebank, Johannesburg 2196, South Africa

The Winter's Tale edited by Baldwin Maxwell published in the
United States of America in Penguin Books 1956
Revised edition published 1971
This new edition edited by Frances E. Dolan published 1999

5 7 9 10 8 6

Copyright © Penguin Books Inc., 1956, 1971
Copyright © Penguin Putnam Inc., 1999
All rights reserved

ISBN 0-14-07.1488-X

Printed in the United States of America
Set in Garamond
Designed by Virginia Norey

Contents

Publisher's Note

IT IS ALMOST half a century since the first volumes of the Pelican Shakespeare appeared under the general editorship of Alfred Harbage. The fact that a new edition, rather than simply a revision, has been undertaken reflects the profound changes textual and critical studies of Shakespeare have undergone in the past twenty years. For the new Pelican series, the texts of the plays and poems have been thoroughly revised in accordance with recent scholarship, and in some cases have been entirely reedited. New introductions and notes have been provided in all the volumes. But the new Shakespeare is also designed as a successor to the original series; the previous editions have been taken into account, and the advice of the previous editors has been solicited where it was feasible to do so.

Certain textual features of the new Pelican Shakespeare should be particularly noted. All lines are numbered that contain a word, phrase, or allusion explained in the glossarial notes. In addition, for convenience, every tenth line is also numbered, in italics when no annotation is indicated. The intrusive and often inaccurate place headings inserted by early editors are omitted (as is becoming standard practice), but for the convenience of those who miss them, an indication of locale now appears as the first item in the annotation of each scene.

In the interest of both elegance and utility, each speech prefix is set in a separate line when the speaker's lines are in verse, except when those words form the second half of a verse line. Thus the verse form of the speech is kept visually intact. What is printed as verse and what is printed as prose has, in general, the authority of the original texts. Departures from the original texts in this regard have only the authority of editorial tradition and the judgment of the Pelican editors; and, in a few instances, are admittedly arbitrary.

The Theatrical World

Economic realities determined the theatrical world in which Shakespeare's plays were written, performed, and received. For centuries in England, the primary theatrical tradition was nonprofessional. Craft guilds (or "mysteries") provided religious drama – mystery plays – as part of the celebration of religious and civic festivals, and schools and universities staged classical and neoclassical drama in both Latin and English as part of their curricula. In these forms, drama was established and socially acceptable. Professional theater, in contrast, existed on the margins of society. The acting companies were itinerant; playhouses could be any available space – the great halls of the aristocracy, town squares, civic halls, inn yards, fair booths, or open fields – and income was sporadic, dependent on the passing of the hat or on the bounty of local patrons. The actors, moreover, were considered little better than vagabonds, constantly in danger of arrest or expulsion.

In the late 1560s and 1570s, however, English professional theater began to gain respectability. Wealthy aristocrats fond of drama – the Lord Admiral, for example, or the Lord Chamberlain – took acting companies under their protection so that the players technically became members of their households and were no longer subject to arrest as homeless or masterless men. Permanent theaters were first built at this time as well, allowing the companies to control and charge for entry to their performances.

Shakespeare's livelihood, and the stunning artistic explosion in which he participated, depended on pragmatic and architectural effort. Professional theater requires ways to restrict access to its offerings; if it does not, and admission fees cannot be charged, the actors do not get paid, the costumes go to a pawnbroker, and there is no such thing as a professional, ongoing theatrical tradition. The answer to that economic need arrived in the late 1560s and 1570s with the creation of the so-called public or amphitheater playhouse. Recent discoveries indicate that the precursor of the Globe playhouse in London (where Shakespeare's mature plays were presented) and the Rose theater (which presented Christopher Marlowe's plays and some of Shakespeare's earliest ones) was the Red Lion theater of 1567. Archaeological studies of the foundations of the Rose and Globe theaters have revealed that the open-air theater of the 1590s and later was probably a polygonal building with fourteen to twenty or twenty-four sides, multistoried, from 75 to 100 feet in diameter, with a raised, partly covered "thrust" stage that projected into a group of standing patrons, or "groundlings," and a covered gallery, seating up to 2,500 or more (very crowded) spectators.

These theaters might have been about half full on any given day, though the audiences were larger on holidays or when a play was advertised, as old and new were, through printed playbills posted around London. The metropolitan area's late-Tudor, early-Stuart population (circa 1590-1620) has been estimated at about 150,000 to 250,000. It has been supposed that in the mid-1590s there were about 15,000 spectators per week at the public theaters; thus, as many as 10 percent of the local population went to the theater regularly. Consequently, the theaters' repertories – the plays available for this experienced and frequent audience – had to change often: in the month between September 15 and October 15, 1595, for instance, the Lord Admiral's Men performed twenty-eight times in eighteen different plays.

Since natural light illuminated the amphitheaters' stages, performances began between noon and two o'clock and ran without a break for two or three hours. They often concluded with a jig, a fencing display, or some other nondramatic exhibition. Weather conditions determined the season for the amphitheaters: plays were performed every day (including Sundays, sometimes, to clerical dismay) except during Lent – the forty days before Easter – or periods of plague, or sometimes during the summer months when law courts were not in session and the most affluent members of the audience were not in London.

To a modern theatergoer, an amphitheater stage like that of the Rose or Globe would appear an unfamiliar mixture of plainness and elaborate decoration. Much of the structure was carved or painted, sometimes to imitate marble; elsewhere, as under the canopy projecting over the stage, to represent the stars and the zodiac. Appropriate painted canvas pictures (of Jerusalem, for example, if the play was set in that city) were apparently hung on the wall behind the acting area, and tragedies were accompanied by black hangings, presumably something like crepe festoons or bunting. Although these theaters did not employ what we would call scenery, early modern spectators saw numerous large props, such as the "bar" at which a prisoner stood during a trial, the "mossy bank" where lovers reclined, an arbor for amorous conversation, a chariot, gallows, tables, trees, beds, thrones, writing desks, and so forth. Audiences might learn a scene's location from a sign (reading "Athens," for example) carried across the stage (as in Bertolt Brecht's twentieth-century productions). Equally captivating (and equally irritating to the theater's enemies) were the rich costumes and personal props the actors used: the most valuable items in the surviving theatrical inventories are the swords, gowns, robes, crowns, and other items worn or carried by the performers.

Magic appealed to Shakespeare's audiences as much as it does to us today, and the theater exploited many deceptive and spectacular devices. A winch in the loft above the stage, called "the heavens," could lower and raise actors playing gods, goddesses, and other supernatural figures to and from the main acting area, just as one or more trapdoors permitted entrances and exits to and from the area, called "hell," beneath the stage. Actors wore elementary makeup such as wigs, false beards, and face paint, and they employed pig's bladders filled with animal blood to make wounds seem more real. They had rudimentary but effective ways of pretending to behead or hang a person. Supernumeraries (stagehands or actors not needed in a particular scene) could make thunder sounds (by shaking a metal sheet or rolling an iron ball down a chute) and show lightning (by blowing inflammable resin through tubes into a flame). Elaborate fireworks enhanced the effects of dragons flying through the air or imitated such celestial phenomena as comets, shooting stars, and multiple suns. Horses' hoofbeats, bells (located perhaps in the tower above the stage), trumpets and drums, clocks, cannon shots and gunshots, and the like were common sound effects. And the music of viols, cornets, oboes, and recorders was a regular feature of theatrical performances.

For two relatively brief spans, from the late 1570s to 1590 and from 1599 to 1614, the amphitheaters competed with the so-called private, or indoor, theaters, which originated as, or later represented themselves as, educational institutions training boys as singers for church services and court performances. These indoor theaters had two features that were distinct from the amphitheaters': their personnel and their playing spaces. The amphitheaters' adult companies included both adult men, who played the male roles, and boys, who played the female roles; the private, or indoor, theater companies, on the other hand, were entirely composed of boys aged about 8 to 16, who were, or could pretend to be, candidates for singers in a church or a royal boys' choir. (Until 1660, professional theatrical companies included no women.) The playing space would appear much more familiar to modern audiences than the long-vanished amphitheaters; the later indoor theaters were, in fact, the ancestors of the typical modern theater. They were enclosed spaces, usually rectangular, with the stage filling one end of the rectangle and the audience arrayed in seats or benches across (and sometimes lining) the building's longer axis. These spaces staged plays less frequently than the public theaters (perhaps only once a week) and held far fewer spectators than the amphitheaters: about 200 to 600, as opposed to 2,500 or more. Fewer patrons mean a smaller gross income, unless each pays more. Not surprisingly, then, private theaters charged higher prices than the amphitheaters, probably sixpence, as opposed to a penny for the cheapest entry.

Protected from the weather, the indoor theaters presented plays later in the day than the amphitheaters, and used artificial illumination – candles in sconces or candelabra. But candles melt, and need replacing, snuffing, and trimming, and these practical requirements may have been part of the reason the indoor theaters introduced breaks in the performance, the intermission so dear to the heart of theatergoers and to the pocketbooks of theater concessionaires ever since. Whether motivated by the need to tend to the candles or by the entrepreneurs' wishing to sell oranges and liquor, or both, the indoor theaters eventually established the modern convention of the non-continuous performance. In the early modern "private" theater, musical performances apparently filled the inter-missions, which in Stuart theater jargon seem to have been called "acts."

At the end of the first decade of the seventeenth century, the distinction between public amphitheaters and private indoor companies ceased. For various cultural, political, and economic reasons, individual companies gained control of both the public, open-air theaters and the indoor ones, and companies mixing adult men and boys took over the formerly "private" theaters. Despite the death of the boys' companies and of their highly innova-tive theaters (for which such luminous playwrights as Ben Jonson, George Chapman, and John Marston wrote), their playing spaces and conventions had an immense im-pact on subsequent plays: not merely for the intervals (which stressed the artistic and architectonic importance of "acts"), but also because they introduced political and social satire as a popular dramatic ingredient, even in tragedy, and a wider range of actorly effects, encouraged by their more intimate playing spaces.

Even the briefest sketch of the Shakespearean theatrical world would be incomplete without some comment on the social and cultural dimensions of theaters and playing in the period. In an intensely hierarchical and status-conscious society, professional actors and their ventures had hardly any respectability; as we have indicated, to protect themselves against laws designed to curb vagabondage and the increase of masterless men, actors resorted to the near-fiction that they were the servants of noble masters, and wore their distinctive livery. Hence the company for which Shakespeare wrote in the 1590s called itself the Lord Chamberlain's Men and pretended that the public, money-getting performances were in fact rehearsals for private performances before that high court official. From 1598, the Privy Council had licensed theatrical companies, and after 1603, with the accession of King James I, the companies gained explicit royal protection, just as the Queen's Men had for a time under Queen Elizabeth. The Chamberlain's Men became the King's Men, and the other companies were patronized by the other members of the royal family.

These designations were legal fictions that half-concealed an important economic and social development, the evolution away from the theater's organization on the model of the guild, a self-regulating confraternity of individual artisans, into a proto-capitalist organization. Shakespeare's company became a joint-stock company, where persons who supplied capital and, in some cases, such as Shakespeare's, capital and talent, employed themselves and others in earning a return on that capital. This development meant that actors and theater companies were outside both the traditional guild structures, which required some form of civic or royal charter, and the feudal household organization of master-and-servant. This anomalous, maverick social and economic condition made theater companies practically unruly and potentially even dangerous; consequently, numerous official bodies – including the London metropolitan and ecclesiastical authorities as well as, occasionally, the royal court itself – tried, without much success, to control and even to disband them.

Public officials had good reason to want to close the theaters: they were attractive nuisances – they drew often riotous crowds, they were always noisy, and they could be politically offensive and socially insubordinate. Until the Civil War, however, anti-theatrical forces failed to shut down professional theater, for many reasons – limited surveillance and few police powers, tensions or outright hostilities among the agencies that sought to check or channel theatrical activity, and lack of clear policies for control. Another reason must have been the theaters' undeniable popularity. Curtailing any activity enjoyed by such a substantial percentage of the population was difficult, as various Roman emperors attempting to limit circuses had learned, and the Tudor-Stuart audience was not merely large, it was socially diverse and included women. The prevalence of public entertainment in this period has been underestimated. In fact, fairs, holidays, games, sporting events, the equivalent of modern parades, freak shows, and street exhibitions all abounded, but the theater was the most widely and frequently available entertainment to which people of every class had access. That fact helps account both for its quantity and for the fear and anger it aroused.

WILLIAM SHAKESPEARE OF STRATFORD-UPON-AVON, GENTLEMAN

Many people have said that we know very little about William Shakespeare's life – pinheads and postcards are often mentioned as appropriately tiny surfaces on which to record the available information. More imaginatively and perhaps more correctly, Ralph Waldo Emerson wrote, "Shakespeare is the only biographer of Shakespeare. . . . So far from Shakespeare's being the least known, he is the one person in all modern history fully known to us."

In fact, we know more about Shakespeare's life than we do about almost any other English writer's of his era. His last will and testament (dated March 25, 1616) survives, as do numerous legal contracts and court documents involving Shakespeare as principal or witness, and parish records in Stratford and London. Shakespeare appears quite often in official records of King James's royal court, and of course Shakespeare's name appears on numerous title pages and in the written and recorded words of his literary contemporaries Robert Greene, Henry Chettle, Francis Meres, John Davies of Hereford, Ben Jonson, and many others. Indeed, if we make due allowance for the bloating of modern, run-of-the-mill bureaucratic records, more information has survived over the past four hundred years about William Shakespeare of Stratford-upon-Avon, Warwickshire, than is likely to survive in the next four hundred years about any reader of these words.

What we do not have are entire categories of information – Shakespeare's private letters or diaries, drafts and revisions of poems and plays, critical prefaces or essays, commendatory verse for other writers' works, or instructions guiding his fellow actors in their performances, for instance – that we imagine would help us understand and appreciate his surviving writings. For all we know, many such data never existed as written records. Many literary and theatrical critics, not knowing what might once have existed, more or less cheerfully accept the situation; some even make a theoretical virtue of it by claiming that such data are irrelevant to understanding and interpreting the plays and poems.

So, what do we know about William Shakespeare, the man responsible for thirty-seven or perhaps more plays, more than 150 sonnets, two lengthy narrative poems, and some shorter poems?

While many families by the name of Shakespeare (or some variant spelling) can be identified in the English Midlands as far back as the twelfth century, it seems likely that the dramatist's grandfather, Richard, moved to Snitterfield, a town not far from Stratford-upon-Avon, sometime before 1529. In Snitterfield, Richard Shakespeare leased farmland from the very wealthy Robert Arden. By 1552, Richard's son John had moved to a large house on Henley Street in Stratford-upon-Avon, the house that stands today as "The Birthplace." In Stratford, John Shakespeare traded as a glover, dealt in wool, and lent money at interest; he also served in a variety of civic posts, including "High Bailiff," the municipality's equivalent of mayor. In 1557, he married Robert Arden's youngest daughter, Mary. Mary and John had four sons – William was the oldest – and four daughters, of whom only Joan outlived her most celebrated sibling. William was baptized (an event entered in the Stratford parish church records) on April 26, 1564, and it has become customary, without any good factual support, to suppose he was born on April 23, which happens to be the feast day of Saint George, patron saint of England, and is also the date on which he died, in 1616. Shakespeare married Anne Hathaway in 1582, when he was eighteen and she was twenty-six; their first child was born five months later. It has been generally assumed that the marriage was enforced and subsequently unhappy, but these are only assumptions; it has been estimated, for instance, that up to one third of Elizabethan brides were pregnant when they married. Anne and William Shakespeare had three children: Susanna, who married a prominent local physician, John Hall; and the twins Hamnet, who died young in 1596, and Judith, who married Thomas Quiney – apparently a rather shady individual. The name Hamnet was unusual but not unique: he and his twin sister were named for their godparents, Shakespeare's neighbors Hamnet and Judith Sadler. Shakespeare's father died in 1601 (the year of *Hamlet*), and Mary Arden Shakespeare died in 1608 (the year of *Coriolanus*). William Shakespeare's last surviving direct descendant was his granddaughter Elizabeth Hall, who died in 1670.

Between the birth of the twins in 1585 and a clear reference to Shakespeare as a practicing London dramatist in Robert Greene's sensationalizing, satiric pamphlet, *Greene's Groatsworth of Wit* (1592), there is no record of where William Shakespeare was or what he was doing. These seven so-called lost years have been imaginatively filled by scholars and other students of Shakespeare: some think he traveled to Italy, or fought in the Low Countries, or studied law or medicine, or worked as an apprentice actor/writer, and so on to even more fanciful possibilities. Whatever the biographical facts for those "lost" years, Greene's nasty remarks in 1592 testify to professional envy and to the fact that Shakespeare already had a successful career in London. Speaking to his fellow playwrights, Greene warns both generally and specifically:

> . . . trust them [actors] not: for there is an upstart crow, beautified with our feathers, that with his tiger's heart wrapped in a player's hide supposes he is as well able to bombast out a blank verse as the best of you; and being an absolute Johannes Factotum, is in his own conceit the only Shake-scene in a country.

The passage mimics a line from *3 Henry VI* (hence the play must have been performed before Greene wrote) and seems to say that "Shake-scene" is both actor and playwright, a jack-of-all-trades. That same year, Henry Chettle protested Greene's remarks in *Kind-Heart's Dream,* and each of the next two years saw the publication of poems – *Venus and Adonis* and *The Rape of Lucrece,* respectively – publicly ascribed to (and dedicated by) Shakespeare. Early in 1595 he was named one of the senior members of a prominent acting company, the Lord Chamberlain's Men, when they received payment for court performances during the 1594 Christmas season.

Clearly, Shakespeare had achieved both success and reputation in London. In 1596, upon Shakespeare's application, the College of Arms granted his father the now-familiar coat of arms he had taken the first steps to obtain almost twenty years before, and in 1598, John's son – now permitted to call himself "gentleman" – took a 10 percent share in the new Globe playhouse. In 1597, he bought a substantial bourgeois house, called New Place, in Stratford – the garden remains, but Shakespeare's house, several times rebuilt, was torn down in 1759 – and over the next few years Shakespeare spent large sums buying land and making other investments in the town and its environs. Though he worked in London, his family remained in Stratford, and he seems always to have considered Stratford the home he would eventually return to. Something approaching a disinterested appreciation of Shakespeare's popular and professional status appears in Francis Meres's *Palladis Tamia* (1598), a not especially imaginative and perhaps therefore persuasive record of literary reputations. Reviewing contemporary English writers, Meres lists the titles of many of Shakespeare's plays, including one not now known, *Love's Labor's Won,* and praises his "mellifluous & hony-tongued" "sugred Sonnets," which were then circulating in manuscript (they were first collected in 1609). Meres describes Shakespeare as "one of the best" English playwrights of both comedy and tragedy. In *Remains . . . Concerning Britain* (1605), William Camden – a more authoritative source than the imitative Meres – calls Shakespeare one of the "most pregnant witts of these our times" and joins him with such writers as Chapman, Daniel, Jonson, Marston, and Spenser. During the first decades of the seventeenth century, publishers began to attribute numerous play quartos, including some non-Shakespearean ones, to Shakespeare, either by name or initials, and we may assume that they deemed Shakespeare's name and supposed authorship, true or false, commercially attractive.

For the next ten years or so, various records show

Shakespeare's dual career as playwright and man of the theater in London, and as an important local figure in Stratford. In 1608-9 his acting company – designated the "King's Men" soon after King James had succeeded Queen Elizabeth in 1603 – rented, refurbished, and opened a small interior playing space, the Blackfriars theater, in London, and Shakespeare was once again listed as a substantial sharer in the group of proprietors of the playhouse. By May 11, 1612, however, he describes himself as a Stratford resident in a London lawsuit – an indication that he had withdrawn from day-to-day professional activity and returned to the town where he had always had his main financial interests. When Shakespeare bought a substantial residential building in London, the Blackfriars Gatehouse, close to the theater of the same name, on March 10, 1613, he is recorded as William Shakespeare "of Stratford upon Avon in the county of Warwick, gentleman," and he named several London residents as the building's trustees. Still, he continued to participate in theatrical activity: when the new Earl of Rutland needed an allegorical design to bear as a shield, or *impresa,* at the celebration of King James's Accession Day, March 24, 1613, the earl's accountant recorded a payment of 44 shillings to Shakespeare for the device with its motto.

For the last few years of his life, Shakespeare evidently concentrated his activities in the town of his birth. Most of the final records concern business transactions in Stratford, ending with the notation of his death on April 23, 1616, and burial in Holy Trinity Church, Stratford-upon-Avon.

THE QUESTION OF AUTHORSHIP

The history of ascribing Shakespeare's plays (the poems do not come up so often) to someone else began, as it continues, peculiarly. The earliest published claim that someone else wrote Shakespeare's plays appeared in an

1856 article by Delia Bacon in the American journal *Putnam's Monthly* – although an Englishman, Thomas Wilmot, had shared his doubts in private (even secretive) conversations with friends near the end of the eighteenth century. Bacon's was a sad personal history that ended in madness and poverty, but the year after her article, she published, with great difficulty and the bemused assistance of Nathaniel Hawthorne (then United States Consul in Liverpool, England), her *Philosophy of the Plays of Shakspere Unfolded.* This huge, ornately written, confusing farrago is almost unreadable; sometimes its intents, to say nothing of its arguments, disappear entirely beneath near-raving, ecstatic writing. Tumbled in with much supposed "philosophy" appear the claims that Francis Bacon (from whom Delia Bacon eventually claimed descent), Walter Ralegh, and several other contemporaries of Shakespeare's had written the plays. The book had little impact except as a ridiculed curiosity.

Once proposed, however, the issue gained momentum among people whose conviction was the greater in proportion to their ignorance of sixteenth- and seventeenth-century English literature, history, and society. Another American amateur, Catherine P. Ashmead Windle, made the next influential contribution to the cause when she published *Report to the British Museum* (1882), wherein she promised to open "the Cipher of Francis Bacon," though what she mostly offers, in the words of S. Schoenbaum, is "demented allegorizing." An entire new cottage industry grew from Windle's suggestion that the texts contain hidden, cryptographically discoverable ciphers – "clues" – to their authorship; and today there are not only books devoted to the putative ciphers, but also pamphlets, journals, and newsletters.

Although Baconians have led the pack of those seeking a substitute Shakespeare, in *"Shakespeare" Identified* (1920), J. Thomas Looney became the first published "Oxfordian" when he proposed Edward de Vere, seventeenth earl of Oxford, as the secret author of Shakespeare's plays. Also for Oxford and his "authorship" there are today dedicated societies, articles, journals, and books. Less popular candidates – Queen Elizabeth and Christopher Marlowe among them – have had adherents, but the movement seems to have divided into two main contending factions, Baconian and Oxfordian. (For further details on all the candidates for "Shakespeare," see S. Schoenbaum, *Shakespeare's Lives*, 2nd ed., 1991.)

The Baconians, the Oxfordians, and supporters of other candidates have one trait in common – they are snobs. Every pro-Bacon or pro-Oxford tract sooner or later claims that the historical William Shakespeare of Stratford-upon-Avon could not have written the plays because he could not have had the training, the university education, the experience, and indeed the imagination or background their author supposedly possessed. Only a learned genius like Bacon or an aristocrat like Oxford could have written such fine plays. (As it happens, lucky male children of the middle class had access to better education than most aristocrats in Elizabethan England – and Oxford was not particularly well educated.) Shakespeare received in the Stratford grammar school a formal education that would daunt many college graduates today; and popular rival playwrights such as the very learned Ben Jonson and George Chapman, both of whom also lacked university training, achieved great artistic success, without being taken as Bacon or Oxford.

Besides snobbery, one other quality characterizes the authorship controversy: lack of evidence. A great deal of testimony from Shakespeare's time shows that Shakespeare wrote Shakespeare's plays and that his contemporaries recognized them as distinctive and distinctly superior. (Some of that contemporary evidence is collected in E. K. Chambers, *William Shakespeare: A Study of Facts and Problems*, 2 vols., 1930.) Since that testimony comes from Shakespeare's enemies and theatrical competitors as well as from his co-workers and from the Elizabethan equivalent of literary journalists, it seems unlikely that, if any one of these sources had known he was a fraud, they would have failed to record that fact.

Books About Shakespeare's Theater

Useful scholarly studies of theatrical life in Shakespeare's day include: G. E. Bentley, *The Jacobean and Caroline Stage,* 7 vols. (1941-68), and the same author's *The Professions of Dramatist and Player in Shakespeare's Time, 1590-1642* (1986); E. K. Chambers, *The Elizabethan Stage,* 4 vols. (1923); R. A. Foakes, *Illustrations of the English Stage, 1580-1642* (1985); Andrew Gurr, *The Shakespearean Stage,* 3rd ed. (1992), and the same author's *Play-going in Shakespeare's London,* 2nd ed. (1996); Edwin Nungezer, *A Dictionary of Actors* (1929); Carol Chillington Rutter, ed., *Documents of the Rose Playhouse* (1984).

Books About Shakespeare's Life

The following books provide scholarly, documented accounts of Shakespeare's life: G. E. Bentley, *Shakespeare: A Biographical Handbook* (1961); E. K. Chambers, *William Shakespeare: A Study of Facts and Problems,* 2 vols. (1930); S. Schoenbaum, *William Shakespeare: A Compact Documentary Life* (1977); and *Shakespeare's Lives,* 2nd ed. (1991), by the same author. Many scholarly editions of Shakespeare's complete works print brief compilations of essential dates and events. References to Shakespeare's works up to 1700 are collected in C. M. Ingleby et al., *The Shakespeare Allusion-Book,* rev. ed., 2 vols. (1932).

The Texts of Shakespeare

As far as we know, only one manuscript conceivably in Shakespeare's own hand may (and even this is much disputed) exist: a few pages of a play called *Sir Thomas More,* which apparently was never performed. What we do have, as later readers, performers, scholars, students, are printed texts. The earliest of these survive in two forms: quartos and folios. Quartos (from the Latin for "four") are small books, printed on sheets of paper that were then folded in fours, to make eight double-sided pages. When these were bound together, the result was a squarish, eminently portable volume that sold for the relatively small sum of sixpence (translating in modern terms to about $5.00). In folios, on the other hand, the sheets are folded only once, in half, producing large, impressive volumes taller than they are wide. This was the format for important works of philosophy, science, theology, and literature (the major precedent for a folio Shakespeare was Ben Jonson's *Works,* 1616). The decision to print the works of a popular playwright in folio is an indication of how far up on the social scale the theatrical profession had come during Shakespeare's lifetime. The Shakespeare folio was an expensive book, selling for between fifteen and eighteen shillings, depending on the binding (in modern terms, from about $150 to $180). Twenty Shakespeare plays of the thirty-seven that survive first appeared in quarto, seventeen of which appeared during Shakespeare's lifetime; the rest of the plays are found only in folio.

The First Folio was published in 1623, seven years after Shakespeare's death, and was authorized by his fellow actors, the co-owners of the King's Men. This publication was certainly a mark of the company's enormous respect for Shakespeare; but it was also a way of turning the old plays, most of which were no longer current in the playhouse, into ready money (the folio includes only Shakespeare's plays, not his sonnets or other nondramatic verse). Whatever the motives behind the publication of the folio, the texts it preserves constitute the basis for almost all later editions of the playwright's works. The texts, however, differ from those of the earlier quartos, sometimes in minor respects but often significantly – most strikingly in the two texts of *King Lear,* but also in important ways in *Hamlet, Othello,* and *Troilus and Cressida.* (The variants are recorded in the textual notes to each play in the new Pelican series.) The differences in these texts represent, in a sense, the essence of theater: the texts of plays were initially not intended for publication. They were scripts, designed for the actors to perform – the principal life of the play at this period was in performance. And it follows that in Shakespeare's theater the playwright typically had no say either in how his play was performed or in the disposition of his text – he was an employee of the company. The authoritative figures in the theatrical enterprise were the shareholders in the company, who were for the most part the major actors. They decided what plays were to be done; they hired the playwright and often gave him an outline of the play they wanted him to write. Often, too, the play was a collaboration: the company would retain a group of writers, and parcel out the scenes among them. The resulting script was then the property of the company, and the actors would revise it as they saw fit during the course of putting it on stage. The resulting text belonged to the company. The playwright had no rights in it once he had been paid. (This system survives largely intact in the movie industry, and most of the playwrights of Shakespeare's time were as anonymous as most screenwriters are today.) The script could also, of course, continue to change as the tastes of audiences and the requirements of the actors changed. Many – perhaps most – plays were revised when they were reintroduced after any substantial absence from the repertory, or when they were performed by a company different from the one that originally commissioned the play.

Shakespeare was an exceptional figure in this world because he was not only a shareholder and actor in his company, but also its leading playwright – he was literally his own boss. He had, moreover, little interest in the publication of his plays, and even those that appeared during his lifetime with the authorization of the company show no signs of any editorial concern on the part of the author. Theater was, for Shakespeare, a fluid and supremely responsive medium – the very opposite of the great classic canonical text that has embodied his works since 1623.

The very fluidity of the original texts, however, has meant that Shakespeare has always had to be edited. Here is an example of how problematic the editorial project inevitably is, a passage from the most famous speech in *Romeo and Juliet,* Juliet's balcony soliloquy beginning "O Romeo, Romeo, wherefore art thou Romeo?" Since the eighteenth century, the standard modern text has read,

> What's Montague? It is nor hand, nor foot,
> Nor arm, nor face, nor any other part
> Belonging to a man. O be some other name!
> What's in a name? That which we call a rose
> By any other name would smell as sweet.
>
> (II.2.40-44)

Editors have three early texts of this play to work from, two quarto texts and the folio. Here is how the First Quarto (1597) reads:

> Whats *Mountague?* It is nor band nor foote,
> Nor arme, nor face, nor any other part.
> Whats in a name? That which we call a Rose,
> By any other name would smell as sweet:

Here is the Second Quarto (1599):

> Whats *Mountague*? it is nor hand nor foote,
> Nor arme nor face, ô be some other name
> Belonging to a man.
> Whats in a name that which we call a rose,
> By any other word would smell as sweete,

And here is the First Folio (1623):

> What's *Mountague*? it is nor hand nor foote,
> Nor arme, nor face, O be some other name
> Belonging to a man.
> What? in a names that which we call a Rose,
> By any other word would smell as sweete,

There is in fact no early text that reads as our modern text does – and this is the most famous speech in the play. Instead, we have three quite different texts, all of which are clearly some version of the same speech, but none of which seems to us a final or satisfactory version. The transcendently beautiful passage in modern editions is an editorial invention: editors have succeeded in conflating and revising the three versions into something we recognize as great poetry. Is this what Shakespeare "really" wrote? Who can say? What we can say is that Shakespeare always had performance, not a book, in mind.

Books About the Shakespeare Texts

The standard study of the printing history of the First Folio is W. W. Greg, *The Shakespeare First Folio* (1955). J. K. Walton, *The Quarto Copy for the First Folio of Shakespeare* (1971), is a useful survey of the relation of the quartos to the folio. The second edition of Charlton Hinman's *Norton Facsimile* of the First Folio (1996), with a new introduction by Peter Blayney, is indispensable. Stanley Wells and Gary Taylor, *William Shakespeare: A Textual Companion,* keyed to the Oxford text, gives a comprehensive survey of the editorial situation for all the plays and poems.

THE GENERAL EDITORS

Introduction

THE WINTER'S TALE IS ONE of Shakespeare's last plays.
First performed early in 1611, it was written then or
shortly before. In it, we encounter many types familiar
from Shakespeare's earlier works: the jealous husband, the
falsely accused wife, the female confidante, the true friend,
the loyal servant whose integrity is such that he can dis-
obey a wrongheaded master, the cross-dressed heroine,
and the beleaguered lovers. Indeed, Shakespeare seems to
sample his career in this play, replaying favorite themes
and recombining reliable characters and conflicts. Yet the
play also includes a host of surprises. Some, such as a Bo-
hemian seacoast, Shakespeare borrows from his source,
Robert Greene's prose romance *Pandosto,* which was first
published in 1588, but had gone through many editions
by the time Shakespeare wrote *The Winter's Tale.* Shakespeare also borrows most of the characters and the basic
situation from Greene; in shaping the character of Autolycus, he may also have drawn on Greene's and Thomas
Harman's pamphlet accounts of vagrant criminals in contemporary England. The range of materials on which
Shakespeare seems to have drawn in composing *The Winter's Tale* suggests the richness and hybridity of this play,
which owes debts to the magical transformations in
Ovid's *Metamorphoses* and the generous sense of possibil-
ity in prose romances, to folktales about abandoned
princesses, to brief, cheap accounts of murdered babies
dumped in London privies, to elaborate masques performed at court, and to street entertainers. Figures of
myth, history, the imagination, and contemporary popular culture share the stage. For instance, Autolycus, ca-
vorting and picking pockets amidst the shepherds of

pastoral fantasy, is a figure from London street life – from the underworld, not the green world.

Many striking elements of *The Winter's Tale* are unique to Shakespeare's vision: the bear, the appearance of Time as a character, Hermione's sixteen-year absence, the sea sickness that prevents Autolycus from making the shepherd (and his story) known to Florizel, a statue that comes to life, Paulina's sudden remarriage. These improbabilities, which might be summed up in the notorious stage direction "*Exit, pursued by a bear*" (III.3.57 s.d.), make it hard for some people to take this play seriously. But perhaps what is most unlikely, but also most moving, is not that a bear will turn up out of nowhere and eat you – which is one way of dramatizing the unexpected assaults of daily life – but that the bear does not eat the baby on whom hope depends; not that one is betrayed or aggrieved, but that one goes on; not that we grow wrinkled, but that love can be renewed and sustained, and that forgiveness can attend a process of loss.

The doomed Mamillius explains, "A sad tale's best for winter" (II.1.25), and the play obliges in its first acts with a very sad winter's tale, indeed. Mamillius's death stands as the closing knell in the play's tragic movement. Leontes concedes after learning of his son's death, "I have too much believed mine own suspicion" (III.2.149). The death of Mamillius, who is so lavishly praised as the hope for the future in the play's first scene, is the one irredeemable consequence of Leontes' unjustified rage. The play then switches in midstream to a spring's tale. Just as spring is born out of the death, decay, and cold of winter, so the renewal in Acts IV and V depends on the injury and loss in the first three acts. When the play was first printed, in the folio of 1623, it was grouped with the comedies. While it may sit uneasily in that company, the play does shift in mood as well as in setting and time in the course of III.3 and IV.1. Whereas the source allows the accused wife to die, and then has the jealous king commit suicide, Shakespeare allows for redemption and reunion. For these to occur, however, the characters need to escape the dark, claustrophobic, anxious court; they need time and space. The action moves not only from Sicilia to Bohemia, but from court to countryside, from royalty to shepherds, who, in a final comic counterturn, will be elevated into gentlemen and royal in-laws. The turning point is Leontes' admission of guilt. Next, Antigonus recounts a dream in which Hermione figures first as a saint, dressed in white "like very sanctity," and then as a shrieking fury who condemns him never to see his wife again; in fulfillment of this prophecy, a bear chases and eats him. The shepherd sums up to his son, as they assess the discovery of Antigonus's gnawed corpse and the foundling baby: "thou met'st with things dying, I with things new-born" (III.3.109-110).

When Time announces that sixteen years have passed, winter has turned to spring. Yet the time references in IV.4 are confused and confusing, perhaps deliberately creating a sense of timelessness. Furthermore, the two seasons and their associations remain in tension to the end. As the sheepshearing begins, Leontes grieves alone and Hermione is dead, or at least in suspended animation. Even in the conclusion, joy and sorrow intermix, renewal contains the reminder of loss.

In its extremes of emotion felt simultaneously, its jumble of images, its improbabilities, the play feels like a dream. Leontes' jealousy has the texture of a nightmare, and turns life for Polixenes and Hermione into a nightmare as well. Nothing is what it seems; the familiar becomes suddenly, terrifyingly strange, yet order is restored as suddenly and surprisingly as it was disturbed. In an exchange between Hermione and Leontes, both agree on the dreamlike quality of their experience.

HERMIONE
    Sir,
    You speak a language that I understand not,

>My life stands in the level of your dreams,
>Which I'll lay down.

LEONTES

>Your actions are my
>dreams.
>You had a bastard by Polixenes,
>And I but dreamed it.

>(III.2.78-83)

Leontes is being snide, yet he unknowingly speaks the truth. He *did* but dream this. Later, Perdita views her time with Florizel, before his father discovers them, as a "dream" from which she's roughly awakened (IV.4.447-48) Perdita's happiness, like that of her parents, suddenly dissolves, proving that experience is unstable and hallucinatory.

If the play is a dream, it is a violent dream, made up of the detritus of deep fears of intimate betrayal, of folklore, and of recent English history. Perdita's story is, for the most part, a fairy tale. At its happy if outlandish conclusion, when she who was lost is found, various characters remark that the play's closing movement is "Like an old tale" (V.3.117; cf. V.2.29, 60). This "old tale" is the story of infant abandonment, whose conventions from antiquity to the Renaissance John Boswell delineates: "The children are of lofty though complicated ancestry; a male figure orders the abandonment, to the regret of the mother; they are actually taken away and left by servants; they are found by shepherds and reared by foster parents; they subsequently rise to greatness" (*The Kindness of Strangers: The Abandonment of Children in Western Europe from Late Antiquity to the Renaissance* [1990], p. 76). In its resolution the story is so wonderful "that ballad-makers cannot be able to express it" (V.2.25-26). But if the play emphasizes its own fantastic and fictional qualities, it also reminds us that folk and fairy tales include grotesque and extreme acts of violence, as do texts that purport to describe what really happened, in the remote or recent past.

Beneath the surface lurks the awareness that the violence of husbands and fathers cannot always be so magically survived, let alone forgiven. *The Winter's Tale* is simultaneously an "old [fairy] tale" about a princess abandoned on the coast of Bohemia with identifying tokens and a cache of gold, and the grislier yet more familiar story of a husband and father whose rage leads to the death of his wife and children.

In Leontes, Shakespeare explores the risks when unbridled power is invested in kings and husbands. Like most of the patriarchs at the center of Shakespearean plays, Leontes is an object of scrutiny and critique. Rather than considering alternatives to a patriarchal system, the play explores the potential for corruption and abuse inherent in the system. What happens when a king, father, and husband misuses his power? What are the costs to his subordinates, his kingdom, himself? By what means might he be redeemed? Leontes is aware of the danger that he might be considered a tyrant. Indeed, he defends himself against this charge by insisting on a trial rather than summary justice: "Let us be cleared / Of being tyrannous, since we so openly / Proceed in justice, which shall have due course" (III.2.4-6). Hermione, however, does not fall for this claim, dismissing the trial as "rigor and not law" (III.2.113). For Leontes, the betrayal he suspects and invents would not only humiliate but destroy him, and would extend from his person to the kingdom. Sixteenth- and seventeenth-century English culture did not clearly or consistently distinguish the personal from the political, the household from the commonwealth. For instance, women who killed their husbands or servants who killed their masters might be charged with petty treason – that is, with an assault on order and authority analogous to an assault on the sovereign. Thus, in these extreme cases, the commonplace analogy between household and commonwealth, domestic patriarch and sovereign, conferred much greater significance on the transgressions of wives and servants. Just as a wife's murder of her husband could be understood as a threat to social order, so a queen's adultery might be seen as a political as well as a personal infidelity, since it would cast doubt on the succession. Thus, however unjustified and excessive, Leontes' rage operates within the logic of a culture that routinely invested the sexual and domestic with profound consequence. He arraigns Hermione for "high treason, in committing adultery with Polixenes, . . . and conspiring with Camillo to take away the life of our sovereign lord the king, [her] royal husband" (III.2.14-17). Intensifying her offense by claiming that she conspired to murder him, he insists that he must imprison her for his own protection: "From our free person she should be confined, / Lest that the treachery of the two fled hence / Be left her to perform" (II.1.194-96). In short, he accuses Hermione not only of misbehaving as a wife but of acting "contrary to the faith and allegiance of a true subject" (III.2.18-19).

Yet, as she points out, her status differs from that of his other subjects: she is "A fellow of the royal bed, which owe / A moiety of the throne, a great king's daughter, / The mother to a hopeful prince" (III.2.37-39). This stature makes her more rather than less vulnerable, however, since it gives her every action greater significance. A queen consort's most important public function is simultaneously very intimate – she must produce an heir, preferably male. Patrilineal succession – a name, a crown, or an estate passing from father to son – depends entirely on the monogamy and fertility of mothers. This is true at every social level, hence the oft-repeated jokes in Shakespearean plays about the inevitably conjectural nature of all paternity. In *The Winter's Tale,* for instance, Leontes greets Florizel by saying, "Your mother was most true to wedlock, prince, / For she did print your royal father off, / Conceiving you" (V.1.124-26). For the most part, fathers must take their wives' fidelity and thus their children's legitimacy on faith. The only proof available is resemblance. Resemblance enables Leontes to claim Mamillius as his own, even when he is otherwise beset by doubts: "they say

we are / Almost as like as eggs" (I.2.130-31). Paulina at-
tempts to win Leontes' acceptance of Perdita by dwelling
on resemblance: "Behold, my lords. / Although the print
be little, the whole matter / And copy of the father"
(II.3.97-98). The fact that Leontes observes and remarks
on Florizel's resemblance to his father suggests that
Leontes still anxiously seeks visible proof of paternity. Yet,
in the end, Leontes must accept the daughter he repudi-
ated as his heir.

However outrageous Leontes' actions, they were not
without precedent in English history. Henry VIII accused
two of his wives, Anne Boleyn and Catherine Howard, of
sexual misconduct on flimsy grounds. Shakespeare does
not tell Henry's story in *The Winter's Tale,* although he did
write a historical romance, *Henry VIII,* around this time.
Still, the charges against and executions of Henry's wives
provide a subtext to the play. Anne Boleyn was accused of
adultery and incest; Catherine Howard of sexual inconti-
nence – that is, having a lover prior to her marriage to the
king. In both cases, Henry construed sexual misconduct
as treason, despite the fact that the treason statutes sug-
gested that an adulterous queen's lover was guilty of treason, but she herself was not. Since Henry wanted to
eliminate wives who failed to produce a male heir, he
needed to accuse them of offenses for which they could be
executed. It was possible to emphasize the political consequences of his wives' infidelity because so much significance was attached to the succession. In both cases,
Henry manipulated existing laws and retroactively passed
legislation that would justify and legitimate his proceed-
ings. Yet Henry's ruthlessness had its costs. The strategy of
accusing his wives of sexual misconduct required him to
admit vulnerability, as both husband and king, in a very
public way. The charges against his wives revealed that
even the king could be betrayed and conspired against by
those closest to him.

This is, of course, Leontes' fantasy: his wife and best
friend plot against him. Leontes' crisis is that he believes

himself to be besieged, betrayed, vulnerable, and humiliated. In "rebellion with himself" (I.2.354), Leontes suspects his subordinates to be "A nest of traitors" (II.3.81). As many critics have noticed, Leontes hysterically runs threats together: the witch, the traitor, the scold, the adulterous, murderous wife, the bastard child, the henpecked husband. The abuse he directs at Paulina in II.2 taps into persistent associations in sixteenth- and seventeenth-century English culture: (1) an assertive woman must have a weak husband, since only one spouse can wear the breeches or rule the roost; (2) a woman who cannot hold her tongue cannot preserve her chastity or refrain from violence; (3) a woman who asserts herself inevitably takes something away from men, effeminizing them and masculinizing herself; (4) domestic and political disobedience imply and promote one another. Like his insistence that Hermione's adultery is treasonous, Leontes' response to Paulina's plainspeaking is both out of control and consistent with dominant ways of construing the threat of the disorderly woman.

Yet Leontes is not afraid of his intimate subordinates only. He also suspects Polixenes, the only other character in the play who is truly his equal. At first their friendship, which began in boyhood, seems a perfect example of the love between men that had been revered since antiquity. Leontes so idealizes their shared boyhood that, as Hermione points out, everything since, especially marriage, seems fallen; in growing up and into relation to women, Polixenes and Leontes were expelled from paradise. Indeed, Leontes' distrust of Polixenes begins with his distrust of Hermione. Leontes mistakes Hermione's kindness to Polixenes for adultery, convincing himself that it is she who mistakes: "You have mistook, my lady, / Polixenes for Leontes" (II.1.81-82). He wants his wife to value his friend as much as he does, but also to love himself more. His rage toward Polixenes, while murderous, lacks the ferocity of what he feels toward Hermione, especially once Polixenes moves out of his reach. If, at the start of the play, Leontes is desperate to keep Polixenes with him, to absorb him into the family, by the end of the play, Leontes has shifted his focus to his marriage. However much he regrets his actions toward his friend, his grief is directed largely toward his lost family. In this the play resembles comedies, which so often privilege marriage over friendship, tracing the sometimes painful process by which young people must surrender or subordinate earlier attachments in order to commit themselves fully to marriage. However, Leontes learns the lesson later, and at greater cost, than the young couples of comedy.

If Leontes' violent response to perceived threats from below and beside is the catalyst of the play's action, the play must find a way to absorb and defuse that violence. Most of the play's characters use euphemisms to occlude Leontes' accountability for various deaths. When a servant announces that Mamillius is "gone," Leontes himself is confused: "How? gone?" The servant must bluntly explain that Mamillius is dead (III.2.143). Throughout the play, characters talk about "loss." Antigonus, for instance, refers to Perdita as "Poor thing, condemned to loss" (II.3.191); "exposed / To loss and what may follow" (III.3.49-50). In Antigonus' dream, Hermione names her baby Perdita – she who has been lost – since she "Is counted lost forever" (III.3.32); the oracle explains that Leontes "shall live without an heir if that which is lost be not found" (III.2.133-34). The vocabulary of losing and finding becomes especially noticeable in the final act. Leontes explains to Perdita and Florizel that he "lost a couple" like them, and "lost" Florizel's father (V.1.132, 134-36). The play's characters hedge about the violence perpetrated against the two children, and Leontes' responsibility for it. Dwelling on Leontes' "losses," the play prepares for forgiveness by helping us to repress our knowledge of his crucial role in "losing" his children. As the play moves out of tragedy and into romance, it displaces blame for his angry repudiation of the baby onto those whom he forces to act as the "thrower[s]-out" of the "poor babe" (III.3.28-29). A bear devours Antigonus, and the whole crew of the ship that carried him and the baby goes down in a wreck: "so that all the instruments which aided to expose the child were even then lost when it was found" (V.2.69-71).

Paulina, however, often intervenes in Leontes' self-protecting euphemisms, drawing him up short with blunt words like "killed" – "Killed? / She I killed? I did so, but thou strikest me / Sorely to say I did" (V.1.16-18). Paulina thus forces Leontes to take responsibility for what he has done, and for its consequences. The play's female characters are generally forthright: Hermione first triggers Leontes' jealousy through speech, then vocally defends herself and opposes Leontes; Perdita enters into debate with Polixenes about nature and art, and more than holds her own in conversations with Florizel. Even in this company, Paulina has a special place. Her speech is presented as annoying, but also efficacious. Paulina acts as a mistress of ceremonies, a role very often played by men, such as the Duke in *Measure for Measure* or Prospero in *The Tempest*. While women also play this role, as does Rosalind in *As You Like It*, Paulina's manipulations reveal that it takes even greater patience, wit, and courage to restore a marriage than it takes to transact it in the first place. One Lord warns Paulina, "you have made fault / I' th' boldness of your speech" (III.2.215-16). Although she apologizes, the first scene of Act V, sixteen years later, finds her both unrepentant and unreformed.

Having attempted, unsuccessfully, to interrupt the course of Leontes' jealousy, Paulina masterminds an elaborate scheme to bring him to a full understanding of what he has done. Paulina is the witness who announces that Hermione is dead, and the community of the play seems to accept this intelligence on her authority. "This news is mortal to the queen. Look down / And see what death is doing" (III.2.146-47); "I say she's dead; I'll swear't" (III.2.201). The play frequently distinguishes between saying and swearing, between expressing an opinion and avowing certainty. At this moment, Paulina's willingness to *swear* that Hermione is dead compels belief. Paulina is the one who prevents Leontes from forgetting, from marrying again, from erasing what he did and starting over. Although she states midway that "What's gone and what's past help / Should be past grief" (III.2.220-21), the unfolding of the plot suggests otherwise. In this play, grief can be salutary, if slow and painful. Time does not heal all wounds, but rather makes it possible to understand fully the nature of the wounds, the extent of the loss and the harm. Forgiveness can only be earned by not forgetting.

It is neither possible nor advisable to dissect the process by which the miraculous ending comes about. Certainly, Paulina plays a crucial role, although it is not clear exactly what it is. She claims enormous authority in her own household: reminding Leontes that "the stone is mine" (V.3.58) and threatening to draw the curtain and withhold the vision of his wife from him (V.3.68). Yet, by whatever means Hermione returns to life, she is more than clay in Paulina's or a sculptor's hands. She claims some agency for herself; the agency she claims is maternal. While it has often been remarked that mothers are conspicuously absent in many of Shakespeare's plays, Hermione is very much present at the beginning and the end of the play. She is on the verge of giving birth when Leontes first solicits her intervention with Polixenes, then mistrusts it; we see her banter realistically with her young son; her complaints about Leontes' mistreatment focus on her privileges as a mother. Her resurrection is as a mother as much as or more than a wife. She speaks her only words at the conclusion to her daughter, claiming that maternal love motivated her endurance: "I, / Knowing by Paulina that the oracle / Gave hope thou wast in being, have preserved / Myself to see the issue" (V.3.125-28). It is important that Hermione is an absence at the structural center of the play, removed from the action as her daughter grows up, falls in love, and arranges her own marriage. Thus, the cost of Hermione's survival is marginalization and exclusion. But Hermione does not stand outside of time. Just as mothers were often associated not only with giving life, but with the body in all its fragility, Hermione stands as a figure for mortality: "Hermione was not so much wrinkled, nothing / So aged as this seems" (V.3.28-29). Leontes could consider remarrying and having a new heir, but Hermione will not have another child. Suffering cannot be smoothed off her face, nor can the lost years be reclaimed.

Yet Hermione's presence seems bountiful and miraculous. While, in her debate with Polixenes, Perdita sternly holds nature and art apart, as opposed and distinct, Hermione brings them together, as she mends so many other contraries. She stands at the intersection of the various belief systems in Sicilia: pagan, Protestant, and Catholic. Apollo's oracle champions her innocence. Her story is also a kind of inversion of the myth of Ceres and Proserpina. According to that myth, the seasons mark the relationship between the mother, Ceres, and her daughter, Proserpina. In the six months of the year that Proserpina spent in the underworld with her husband, Dis (Pluto), her mother mourned for her, and decay and death overtook the earth. In the months when mother and daughter could be together, Ceres rejoiced and the earth bloomed anew. In *The Winter's Tale,* the winter of Sicilia in the first acts is imposed not only by the father's harsh jealousy, but by the mother's grief. Yet, the abundant spring in Bohemia does not coincide with the daughter's reunion with her mother. Indeed, Bohemia, however warm and fecund, is a world without any mothers at all. Hermione is removed from the active cycle of mourning and rejoicing that characterizes Ceres; she is more idol than goddess.

When Paulina displays Hermione's statue, she presents her as a kind of saint, who should evoke wonder and reverence. Reformers of the church in the sixteenth century denounced the adoration of saints as idolatrous; images of female saints seem to have been especially vulnerable to iconoclasm. Shakespeare's presentation of Hermione at the end of *The Winter's Tale* suggests that some affection may have lingered for the approachable female intercessors of Catholic piety. Like them, Hermione brings together opposites. Long dead, saints might yet intervene to help the living. Represented by inanimate objects, such as statues or relics, they were simultaneously symbols and agents who could effect change. Similarly, Hermione is both dead and alive, in the past and in the present, remote and warm. She bridges the dead and the living, past and present, those lost and those who still love them. Speaking frequently of "grace," the play's word for beneficence that is unexpected and unearned, Hermione lives to see her daughter, too, become "graceful." Time describes Perdita as "grown in grace / Equal with wondering" (IV.1.24-25). One of the gentlemen recounting the reunion of Polixenes and Leontes, and the recognition of Perdita, says of the visit to the statue: "Every wink of an eye some new grace will be born" (V.2.108-9). While the play cannot be neatly aligned with any particular religion, it does convey a belief in, or at least a hope of, "grace" – good fortune that exceeds our desert.

The Winter's Tale can be viewed as a revision of *Othello,* for in it a similar conflict and cast find comic rather than tragic resolution. The wrongly accused wife is vindicated and restored; the outspoken woman does not die; the hero learns and grows, rather than killing himself. Why can this play work out so much better than *Othello* does? Genre, of course. But the question of genre is connected to the grace that pervades the play, for it is grace that lifts the doom and opens up the horizons of a dark, cramped, cold, tragic world. Time is also crucial to the difference in genre. While the time frame of *Othello* is sharply compressed, leaving no time for reflection or doubt, the "wide gap of time" here expands possibilities. The duration in the play also makes it possible to conjoin the generational concerns of both tragedy and comedy. Shakespearean comedy generally attends to marriageable young people as they define their identities and make matches. Their parents are sometimes obstacles, but most often irrelevant. Shakespearean tragedy often considers conflicts between the generations, as well as the ways in which parental grievances and failures haunt and blight the next generation. In *The Winter's Tale,* we are invited to care equally about the marriageable young people, and their estranged parents, about how parental mistakes shape children's options, but also how children can make "old hearts fresh" (I.1.38).

In fact, the two generations, and the two plots, are not neatly separate. When Leontes, upon meeting Perdita and Florizel, claims that he "lost a couple" like them, he refers, of course, to his own lost children; Florizel and Mamillius were only a month apart in age (V.1.132-34). But given that we are told that Perdita resembles her mother, and Florizel his father, Polixenes, Leontes also faces the images of the wife and friend he lost so many years ago. The strangers from far away turn out to be his own daughter and the son of his best friend. The promise of the future is an image of the past.

FRANCES E. DOLAN
Miami University

Note on the Text

THE FIRST PRINTING OF *The Winter's Tale* was the folio of 1623 (referred to below as F). Therefore, it is one of those plays that might not have survived if this folio, often referred to as the First Folio or first edition of Shakespeare's collected works, had not been printed. *The Winter's Tale* was presented as the last of the comedies. The text, which is generally considered to be clean and reliable, may have been set from a transcript prepared by Ralph Crane. Crane was a scrivener associated with the King's Men, Shakespeare's company of actors; while several of Crane's transcriptions of play texts survive, it is impossible to know the state or provenance of the manuscript on which Crane based his transcription.

The folio printing of this play provides very few stage directions; some have been added here. The folio also tends to begin each scene with a list of all the characters who will appear in the course of that scene, with no indication of exactly when they enter. This edition instead mentions characters as they appear. The act-scene divisions indicated in the margins follow those in the folio. Except for routine standardization and modernization, departures from the folio text are listed below, with the adopted reading in italics followed by the folio reading in roman.

The Names of the Actors (printed at the end of the play in F)

I.1 27 *have* hath
I.2 105 *And* A 125 *heifer* Heycfer 159 *ornaments* ornament; *do* do's 208 *you, they say* say you say 232 *th'entreaties* the Entreaties 254 *forth. In* forth in 276 *hobbyhorse* Holy-Horse 312 *Ay* I 376 *not? Be . . . me,* 'Tis Be . . . me, 'tis 461 *off, hence:* off hence.

II.1 **32 s.d.** (appears before l.1 in F)   **104** *afar off* a farre-off   **136** *Than* then   **182** *have* hane

II.2 **4 s.d.** (appears before l.1 in F)   **53** *let't* le't

II.3 **4** *th' adulteress* th' Adultresse   **26 s.d.** (appears before l.1 in F)   **39** *What* Who   **60** *good, so* good so

III.2 **10** *Silence!* (appears as s.d. in F)   **s.d.** (appears before l.1 in F)   **32** *Who* Whom   **122 s.d.** (appears before l.1 in F)   **235–36** *unto / Our . . . perpetual. Once* (unto / Our shame perpetuall) once

III.3 **48** *begins. Poor* beginnes, poore   **57 s.d.** *Shepherd* (appears before l.1 in F)   **75 s.d.** (appears before l.1 in F)   **115** *made* mad

IV.2 **55 s.d.** *Exeunt* Exit

IV.3 **7** *on* an   **10** *With . . . thrush* With heigh, the Thrush   **37** *currants* currence   **54** *offends* offend

IV.4 **s.d.** (Autolycus enters here in F)   **2** *Do* Do's   **12** *Digest it* Digest   **13** *swoon* sworne   **40** *dearest* deer'st   **54 s.d.** (appears before l.1 in F)   **98** *your* you   **105** *wi' th'* with'   **244** *kiln hole* kill-hole   **296** *Get . . . go* (not assigned in F)   **360** *who* whom   **418** *acknowledged* acknowledge   **422** *who* whom   **427** *shalt* shalt never   **438** *hoop* hope   **466** *your* my   **489** *hide* hides   **522–23** *direction. / If . . . project / May . . . alteration, on* direction, / If . . . project / May . . . alteration. On   **541–42** *follows: if . . . purpose / But . . . flight, make* followes, if . . . purpose / But . . . flight; make   **548** *the son* there Sonne   **667 s.d.** *Exeunt* Exit   **732** *or toaze* at toaze   **741** *pheasant, cock* Pheazant Cock   **836 s.d.** *Exit* Exeunt

V.1 **6** *Whilst* Whilest   **59** *(Where . . . now) appear soul-vexed* (Where . . . now appeare) Soule-vext   **61** *just cause* just such cause   **123 s.d.** *Florizel, Perdita* (appears before l.1 in F)   **160** *his, parting* his parting   **169** *whilst* whilest

V.2 **21** *haply* happily   **62** *This* I his   **68** *Wrecked* Wrackt   **110 s.d.** *Exeunt* Exit

V.3 **18** *Lonely* lovely   **20 s.d.** *(Hermione like a statue* appears before l.1 in F; *Paulina* has no s.d. here in F)   **67** *fixture* fixure   **96** *Or* On

The Winter's Tale

THE NAMES OF THE ACTORS

LEONTES, *King of Sicilia*
MAMILLIUS, *young Prince of Sicilia*
CAMILLO ⎫
ANTIGONUS ⎬ *four lords of Sicilia*
CLEOMENES ⎪
DION ⎭
POLIXENES, *King of Bohemia*
FLORIZEL, *Prince of Bohemia*
ARCHIDAMUS, *a lord of Bohemia*
OLD SHEPHERD, *reputed father of Perdita*
CLOWN, *his son*
AUTOLYCUS, *a rogue*
[A MARINER]
[A JAILER]
HERMIONE, *Queen to Leontes*
PERDITA, *daughter to Leontes and Hermione*
PAULINA, *wife to Antigonus*
EMILIA, *a lady [attending on Hermione]*
[MOPSA ⎫ *shepherdesses*]
[DORCAS ⎭
OTHER LORDS AND GENTLEMEN, [LADIES,
   OFFICERS, AND] SERVANTS, SHEPHERDS, AND
   SHEPHERDESSES
[TIME, AS CHORUS]

[SCENE: *Sicilia and Bohemia*]
*

The Winter's Tale

❧ **I.1.** *Enter Camillo and Archidamus.*

ARCHIDAMUS   If you shall chance, Camillo, to visit Bohemia on the like occasion whereon my services are now on foot, you shall see, as I have said, great differ- 3 ence betwixt our Bohemia and your Sicilia.

CAMILLO   I think this coming summer the King of Sicilia means to pay Bohemia the visitation which he justly owes him.

ARCHIDAMUS   Wherein our entertainment shall shame us, we will be justified in our loves; for indeed – 9

CAMILLO   Beseech you – 10

ARCHIDAMUS   Verily, I speak it in the freedom of my knowledge. We cannot with such magnificence – in so rare – I know not what to say. We will give you sleepy drinks, that your senses, unintelligent of our insufficience, may, though they cannot praise us, as little accuse us.

CAMILLO   You pay a great deal too dear for what's given freely.

ARCHIDAMUS   Believe me, I speak as my understanding instructs me and as mine honesty puts it to utterance. 20

CAMILLO   Sicilia cannot show himself overkind to Bohemia. They were trained together in their childhoods, and there rooted betwixt them then such an affection which cannot choose but branch now. Since their more 24

I.1 In or near Leontes' palace   **3** *on foot* afoot (i.e., if you accompany your master to Bohemia, as I have mine to Sicilia)   **9** *justified* vindicated (as truly welcoming)   **24** *branch* flourish

mature dignities and royal necessities made separation
26 of their society, their encounters, though not personal,
have been royally attorneyed with interchange of gifts,
28 letters, loving embassies; that they have seemed to be
29 together, though absent; shook hands, as over a vast;
30 and embraced, as it were, from the ends of opposed
winds. The heavens continue their loves!

ARCHIDAMUS   I think there is not in the world either mal-
ice or matter to alter it. You have an unspeakable comfort of your young prince Mamillius. It is a gentleman
of the greatest promise that ever came into my note.

CAMILLO   I very well agree with you in the hopes of him.
37 It is a gallant child – one that indeed physics the subject, makes old hearts fresh. They that went on crutches
ere he was born desire yet their life to see him a man.

40 ARCHIDAMUS   Would they else be content or die?

CAMILLO   Yes – if there were no other excuse why they
should desire to live.

ARCHIDAMUS   If the king had no son, they would desire
to live on crutches till he had one.   *Exeunt.*

*

✺ **I.2** *Enter Leontes, Hermione, Mamillius, Polixenes,*
Camillo, Lords.

POLIXENES
1   Nine changes of the watery star hath been
2   The shepherd's note since we have left our throne
3   Without a burden. Time as long again
    Would be filled up, my brother, with our thanks,
    And yet we should, for perpetuity,
6   Go hence in debt. And therefore, like a cipher,

26–27 *not personal . . . attorneyed* not in person (have been carried out by
their agents)   28 *that* so that   29 *vast* wide expanse   37 *physics* cures (presumably of melancholy)
  I.2 The same   1 *watery star* moon   2 *note* observation   3 *Without a burden* empty   3–6 *Time . . . debt* (I could spend another nine months thank-
ing you and still be in your debt forever)   6 *cipher* zero

Yet standing in rich place, I multiply
With one "We thank you" many thousands more
That go before it.   10
LEONTES   Stay your thanks a while
And pay them when you part.
POLIXENES   Sir, that's tomorrow.
I am questioned by my fears of what may chance   12
Or breed upon our absence, that may blow
No sneaping winds at home to make us say,   14
"This is put forth too truly." Besides, I have stayed   15
To tire your royalty.
LEONTES   We are tougher, brother,
Than you can put us to't.
POLIXENES   No longer stay.
LEONTES
One sev'night longer.
POLIXENES   Very sooth, tomorrow.
LEONTES
We'll part the time between's then, and in that
I'll no gainsaying.   20
POLIXENES   Press me not, beseech you, so.
There is no tongue that moves, none, none i' th' world,
So soon as yours could win me. So it should now
Were there necessity in your request, although
'Twere needful I denied it. My affairs
Do even drag me homeward, which to hinder
Were in your love a whip to me, my stay   26
To you a charge and trouble. To save both,
Farewell, our brother.
LEONTES   Tongue-tied our queen? Speak
you.
HERMIONE
I had thought, sir, to have held my peace until
You had drawn oaths from him not to stay. You, sir,   30
Charge him too coldly. Tell him you are sure

---

12 *questioned* worried   14 *sneaping* biting   15 *"This . . . truly"* I had good
reason to worry and to wish myself back home   26 *in* i.e., to make

All in Bohemia's well; this satisfaction
33   The bygone day proclaimed. Say this to him,
34   He's beat from his best ward.
LEONTES   Well said, Hermione.
HERMIONE
      To tell he longs to see his son were strong.
      But let him say so then, and let him go;
      But let him swear so, and he shall not stay,
      We'll thwack him hence with distaffs.
      Yet of your royal presence I'll adventure
40   The borrow of a week. When at Bohemia
      You take my lord, I'll give him my commission
42   To let him there a month behind the gest
43   Prefixed for's parting. Yet, good deed, Leontes,
44   I love thee not a jar o' th' clock behind
45   What lady she her lord. You'll stay?
POLIXENES   No, madam.
HERMIONE
      Nay, but you will?
POLIXENES   I may not, verily.
HERMIONE
      Verily?
48   You put me off with limber vows, but I,
      Though you would seek t' unsphere the stars with oaths,
50   Should yet say, "Sir, no going." Verily,
      You shall not go. A lady's "Verily" is
      As potent as a lord's. Will you go yet?
      Force me to keep you as a prisoner,
54   Not like a guest, so you shall pay your fees
      When you depart and save your thanks. How say you?
      My prisoner or my guest? By your dread "Verily,"
      One of them you shall be.

---

33 *bygone day proclaimed* we received yesterday 34 *ward* defense 42 *let him* let him remain; *gest* place and time of a visit 43 *good deed* indeed 44 *jar* tick 45 *What lady she* any lady 48 *limber* feeble 54 *fees* payments that jailers usually demanded of prisoners upon their release

POLIXENES   Your guest, then, madam.
　To be your prisoner should import offending,   58
　Which is for me less easy to commit
　Than you to punish.   60
HERMIONE   Not your jailer, then,
　But your kind hostess. Come, I'll question you
　Of my lord's tricks and yours when you were boys.
　You were pretty lordings then?
POLIXENES   We were, fair queen,
　Two lads that thought there was no more behind
　But such a day tomorrow as today,
　And to be boy eternal.
HERMIONE   Was not my lord
　The verier wag o' th' two?
POLIXENES
　We were as twinned lambs that did frisk i' th' sun,
　And bleat the one at th' other. What we changed   69
　Was innocence for innocence; we knew not   70
　The doctrine of ill-doing, nor dreamed
　That any did. Had we pursued that life,
　And our weak spirits ne'er been higher reared
　With stronger blood, we should have answered heaven
　Boldly "Not guilty," the imposition cleared
　Hereditary ours.   76
HERMIONE   By this we gather
　You have tripped since.
POLIXENES   O my most sacred lady,
　Temptations have since then been born to's, for
　In those unfledged days was my wife a girl;
　Your precious self had then not crossed the eyes   80
　Of my young playfellow.   81

---

58 *import offending* i.e., imply that I had committed an offense   **69** *changed*
exchanged   **76–77** *the imposition . . . ours* freed even from original sin

HERMIONE   Grace to boot!
Of this make no conclusion, lest you say
Your queen and I are devils. Yet go on.
Th' offenses we have made you do we'll answer,
If you first sinned with us and that with us
You did continue fault and that you slipped not
With any but with us.
LEONTES   Is he won yet?
HERMIONE
He'll stay, my lord.
LEONTES   At my request he would not.
Hermione, my dearest, thou never spok'st
90   To better purpose.
HERMIONE   Never?
LEONTES   Never but once.
HERMIONE
What? Have I twice said well? When was't before?
I prithee tell me. Cram's with praise, and make's
93   As fat as tame things. One good deed dying tongueless
Slaughters a thousand waiting upon that.
Our praises are our wages. You may ride's
With one soft kiss a thousand furlongs ere
97   With spur we heat an acre. But to the goal.
My last good deed was to entreat his stay.
What was my first? It has an elder sister,
100   Or I mistake you. O, would her name were Grace!
But once before I spoke to the purpose. When?
Nay, let me have't; I long.
LEONTES   Why, that was when
103   Three crabbèd months had soured themselves to death
Ere I could make thee open thy white hand

---

81 *Grace to boot* heaven help me (This is the first of many times Hermione refers to grace. It can mean, as here, heaven; it can also refer to an attribute that makes a person attractive and pleasing; acceptance; good fortune granted by God, the gods, or providence as a free and unmerited favor; a human capacity for forgiveness and generous goodwill.)   **93–94** *One . . . that* withholding praise of one good deed discourages a thousand others   **97** *heat* race; *to the goal* to come to the point   **103** *crabbèd* bitter

And clap thyself my love. Then didst thou utter   105
"I am yours forever."
HERMIONE   'Tis grace indeed.
Why, lo you now, I have spoke to the purpose twice;
The one forever earned a royal husband,
Th' other for some while a friend.   109
    [Gives her hand to Polixenes, and they walk apart.]
LEONTES *[Aside]*   Too hot, too hot!
To mingle friendship far is mingling bloods.   *110*
I have *tremor cordis* on me. My heart dances,   111
But not for joy, not joy. This entertainment   112
May a free face put on, derive a liberty
From heartiness, from bounty, fertile bosom,
And well become the agent. 'T may, I grant.
But to be paddling palms and pinching fingers,   116
As now they are, and making practiced smiles
As in a looking glass, and then to sigh, as 'twere
The mort o' th' deer – O, that is entertainment   119
My bosom likes not, nor my brows. Mamillius,   120
Art thou my boy?   121
MAMILLIUS   Ay, my good lord.
LEONTES   I' fecks!
Why, that's my bawcock. What, hast smutched thy nose?   122
They say it is a copy out of mine. Come, captain,
We must be neat – not neat but cleanly, captain.
And yet the steer, the heifer, and the calf
Are all called neat. – Still virginaling   126
Upon his palm? – How now, you wanton calf?
Art thou my calf?

---

105 *clap* pledge   109 *friend* (can also mean "lover")   111 *tremor cordis* heart
palpitations   112–15 *This . . . agent* Hermione's gracious entertainment
may well become her if it be due to a hospitable and generous nature   116
paddling caressing   119 *mort o' th' deer* hunter's horn announcing the death
of the deer   120 *brows* (this is the first of Leontes' many references to the
proverbial claim that betrayed husbands, called cuckolds, sprouted horns on
their foreheads)   121 *I' fecks* in faith   122 *bawcock* fine fellow; *smutched*
smudged   126 *neat* (1) tidy, (2) horned cattle; *virginaling* playing (with fingers)

MAMILLIUS   Yes, if you will, my lord.

LEONTES

129   Thou want'st a rough pash and the shoots that I have,
130   To be full like me; yet they say we are
       Almost as like as eggs. Women say so,
       That will say anything. But were they false
133   As o'erdyed blacks, as wind, as waters, false
       As dice are to be wished by one that fixes
135   No bourn 'twixt his and mine, yet were it true
       To say this boy were like me. Come, sir page,
137   Look on me with your welkin eye. Sweet villain!
138   Most dear'st! my collop! Can thy dam? – may't be? –
139   Affection, thy intention stabs the center!
140   Thou dost make possible things not so held,
       Communicat'st with dreams – how can this be? –
142   With what's unreal thou coactive art,
143   And fellow'st nothing. Then 'tis very credent
       Thou may'st co-join with something; and thou dost,
145   And that beyond commission, and I find it,
       And that to the infection of my brains
       And hard'ning of my brows.

POLIXENES   What means Sicilia?

HERMIONE

       He something seems unsettled.

POLIXENES   How, my lord?

LEONTES

149   What cheer? How is't with you, best brother?

---

129 *pash* head; *shoots* horns   **133** *o'erdyed blacks* (1) Africans, whose dark skin was thought to be a consequence of their closer proximity and greater exposure to the sun, and who, like women, were often considered fickle, lustful, and false, (2) fabrics darkened but also weakened by repeated dyeing   **135** *bourn* boundary   **137** *welkin* sky blue   **138** *collop* small portion   **139** *intention* intensity   **140** *not ... held* not usually considered so   **142** *thou ... art* you collaborate   **143** *fellow'st* befriend; *credent* believable   **145** *commission* what is permitted   **149** *What cheer ... brother* (many editors assign these words to Polixenes)

HERMIONE   You look
   As if you held a brow of much distraction.   *150*
   Are you moved, my lord?
LEONTES   No, in good earnest.
   How sometimes nature will betray its folly,
   Its tenderness, and make itself a pastime
   To harder bosoms! Looking on the lines
   Of my boy's face, methoughts I did recoil   155
   Twenty-three years, and saw myself unbreeched,   156
   In my green velvet coat, my dagger muzzled
   Lest it should bite its master and so prove,
   As ornaments oft do, too dangerous.
   How like, methought, I then was to this kernel,   *160*
   This squash, this gentleman. Mine honest friend,
   Will you take eggs for money?   162
MAMILLIUS   No, my lord, I'll fight.
LEONTES
   You will? Why, happy man be's dole! My brother,   163
   Are you so fond of your young prince as we
   Do seem to be of ours?
POLIXENES   If at home, sir,
   He's all my exercise, my mirth, my matter,
   Now my sworn friend and then mine enemy,
   My parasite, my soldier, statesman, all.
   He makes a July's day short as December,
   And with his varying childness cures in me   *170*
   Thoughts that would thick my blood.   171
LEONTES   So stands this squire
   Officed with me. We two will walk, my lord,
   And leave you to your graver steps. Hermione,
   How thou lov'st us, show in our brother's welcome.
   Let what is dear in Sicily be cheap.

---

155 *methoughts* it seemed to me   156 *unbreeched* before I was old enough to wear distinctively male clothing (small boys and girls both wore the same kind of smock)   162 *take . . . money* be imposed upon   163 *dole* lot   171 *thick my blood* make me melancholy

Next to thyself and my young rover, he's

177 Apparent to my heart.

HERMIONE   If you would seek us,
We are yours i' th' garden. Shall's attend you there?

LEONTES
To your own bents dispose you. You'll be found,
180 Be you beneath the sky. *[Aside]* I am angling now,
Though you perceive me not how I give line.
Go to, go to!

183 How she holds up the neb, the bill to him,
And arms her with the boldness of a wife
185 To her allowing husband!
                    [Exeunt Polixenes, Hermione, and Attendants.]
                    Gone already!
186 Inch-thick, knee-deep, o'er head and ears a forked one!
Go play, boy, play. Thy mother plays, and I
188 Play too, but so disgraced a part, whose issue
Will hiss me to my grave. Contempt and clamor
190 Will be my knell. Go play, boy, play. There have been,
Or I am much deceived, cuckolds ere now;
And many a man there is, even at this present,
Now while I speak this, holds his wife by th' arm,
194 That little thinks she has been sluiced in's absence
And his pond fished by his next neighbor, by
Sir Smile, his neighbor. Nay, there's comfort in't
Whiles other men have gates and those gates opened,
As mine, against their will. Should all despair
That have revolted wives, the tenth of mankind
200 Would hang themselves. Physic for't there's none.
201 It is a bawdy planet, that will strike
Where 'tis predominant; and 'tis powerful, think it,
From east, west, north, and south. Be it concluded,

---

177 *Apparent* heir apparent   183 *neb* face   185 *allowing* approving   186
forked one horned one (cuckold)   188 *whose issue* the result of which   194
sluiced covered or filled with water (i.e., "hosed")   201–2 *It is . . . predominant* (1) wives' unchastity is like a planet that will wreak havoc when it is in
the ascendant, (2) unchaste wives also make the whole planet bawdy

No barricado for a belly. Know't,   204
It will let in and out the enemy
With bag and baggage. Many thousand on's   206
Have the disease and feel't not. How now, boy?

MAMILLIUS
    I am like you, they say.

LEONTES   Why, that's some comfort.
    What, Camillo there?

CAMILLO
    Ay, my good lord.   210

LEONTES
    Go play, Mamillius. Thou'rt an honest man.
                            [Exit Mamillius.]
    Camillo, this great sir will yet stay longer.

CAMILLO
    You had much ado to make his anchor hold;
    When you cast out, it still came home.   214

LEONTES   Didst note it?

CAMILLO
    He would not stay at your petitions, made
    His business more material

LEONTES   Didst perceive it?
        [Aside]
    They're here with me already, whisp'ring, rounding   217
    "Sicilia is a so-forth." 'Tis far gone,
    When I shall gust it last. How came't, Camillo,   219
    That he did stay?   220

CAMILLO   At the good queen's entreaty.

LEONTES
    At the queen's be't. "Good" should be pertinent;
    But so it is, it is not. Was this taken   222
    By any understanding pate but thine?

---

204 *No . . . belly* no way to block access to a womb   206 *on's* of us   214 *still* always   217 *rounding* muttering   217–218 *They're here . . . so-forth* people are already mocking me, whispering I am a "you know what" (perhaps Leontes, unable to say "cuckold," puts two fingers to his head to suggest horns)   219 *gust* realize   222 *so* as; *taken* recognized

224   For thy conceit is soaking, will draw in
       More than the common blocks. Not noted, is't,
226   But of the finer natures, by some severals
227   Of headpiece extraordinary? Lower messes
228   Perchance are to this business purblind? Say.

CAMILLO
       Business, my lord? I think most understand
230   Bohemia stays here longer.

LEONTES   Ha?

CAMILLO   Stays here longer.

LEONTES
       Ay, but why?

CAMILLO
       To satisfy your highness and th' entreaties
233   Of our most gracious mistress.

LEONTES   Satisfy
       Th' entreaties of your mistress? Satisfy;
       Let that suffice. I have trusted thee, Camillo,
       With all the nearest things to my heart, as well
       My chamber councils, wherein, priestlike, thou
       Hast cleansed my bosom, I from thee departed
       Thy penitent reformed. But we have been
240   Deceived in thy integrity, deceived
       In that which seems so.

CAMILLO   Be it forbid, my lord!

LEONTES
242   To bide upon't, thou art not honest; or,
       If thou inclin'st that way, thou art a coward,
244   Which hoxes honesty behind, restraining
       From course required; or else thou must be counted
246   A servant grafted in my serious trust
       And therein negligent; or else a fool

---

224 *conceit is soaking* understanding is absorbing 226 *severals* individuals
227 *Lower messes* inferior men (who at table occupy lower seats) 228 *purblind* wholly blind 233 *Satisfy* (Leontes fixes upon the sexual connotation)
242 *bide* dwell 244 *hoxes* disables 246 *grafted . . . trust* insinuated into my confidence

That seest a game played home, the rich stake drawn,
And tak'st it all for jest.

CAMILLO   My gracious lord,
I may be negligent, foolish, and fearful.   *250*
In every one of these no man is free,
But that his negligence, his folly, fear,
Among the infinite doings of the world,
Sometime puts forth. In your affairs, my lord,   *254*
If ever I were willful-negligent,
It was my folly; if industriously   *256*
I played the fool, it was my negligence,
Not weighing well the end; if ever fearful
To do a thing where I the issue doubted,
Whereof the execution did cry out   *260*
Against the nonperformance, 'twas a fear
Which oft infects the wisest. These, my lord,
Are such allowed infirmities that honesty
Is never free of. But, beseech your grace,
Be plainer with me; let me know my trespass
By its own visage. If I deny it,
'Tis none of mine.

LEONTES   Ha' not you seen, Camillo –
But that's past doubt, you have, or your eye-glass   *268*
Is thicker than a cuckold's horn – or heard –   *269*
For to a vision so apparent rumor   *270*
Cannot be mute – or thought – for cogitation
Resides not in that man that does not think –
My wife is slippery? If thou wilt confess,
Or else be impudently negative,
To have nor eyes nor ears nor thought, then say
My wife's a hobbyhorse, deserves a name   *276*

---

254 *puts forth* reveals itself   **256** *industriously* willfully   **268** *eye-glass* lens of the eye   **269** *thicker* more opaque   **276** *hobbyhorse* a slut, a woman who could be ridden by anybody (in a morris dance, a popular pastime, one person dressed as the hobbyhorse, frisking about in imitation of a horse and presiding over the festivities)

277   As rank as any flax wench that puts to
278   Before her trothplight. Say't and justify't.

CAMILLO
      I would not be a stander-by to hear
280   My sovereign mistress clouded so, without
281   My present vengeance taken. 'Shrew my heart,
      You never spoke what did become you less
283   Than this, which to reiterate were sin
      As deep as that, though true.

LEONTES   Is whispering nothing?
      Is leaning cheek to cheek? Is meeting noses?
286   Kissing with inside lip? stopping the career
      Of laughter with a sigh? – a note infallible
288   Of breaking honesty! – horsing foot on foot?
      Skulking in corners? wishing clocks more swift?
290   Hours, minutes? noon, midnight? and all eyes
291   Blind with the pin and web but theirs, theirs only,
      That would unseen be wicked? Is this nothing?
      Why, then the world and all that's in't is nothing,
      The covering sky is nothing, Bohemia nothing,
      My wife is nothing, nor nothing have these nothings,
      If this be nothing.

CAMILLO   Good my lord, be cured
297   Of this diseased opinion, and betimes,
      For 'tis most dangerous.

LEONTES   Say it be, 'tis true.

CAMILLO
      No, no, my lord.

LEONTES   It is. You lie, you lie.
300   I say thou liest, Camillo, and I hate thee,
      Pronounce thee a gross lout, a mindless slave,

---

277 *flax wench* a woman who worked with flax, a cheap fiber used in making
cloth (more generally, any female worker)   278 *trothplight* engagement
281 *present* immediate; *'Shrew* beshrew, curse   283–84 *which . . . true* to re-
peat the charge against her would be a sin as great as her infidelity were she
guilty   286 *career* full gallop   288 *honesty* chastity; *Horsing . . . on foot* playing footsie   291 *pin and web* cataract   297 *betimes* at once

Or else a hovering temporizer, that   302
Canst with thine eyes at once see good and evil,
Inclining to them both. Were my wife's liver
Infected as her life, she would not live
The running of one glass.   306

CAMILLO   Who does infect her?

LEONTES
Why, he that wears her like her medal, hanging
About his neck – Bohemia, who, if I
Had servants true about me that bare eyes   309
To see alike mine honor as their profits,   310
Their own particular thrifts, they would do that
Which should undo more doing. Ay, and thou,
His cupbearer – whom I from meaner form   313
Have benched and reared to worship, who may'st see   314
Plainly as heaven sees earth and earth sees heaven,
How I am gall'd – might'st bespice a cup
To give mine enemy a lasting wink,
Which draft to me were cordial.

CAMILLO   Sir, my lord,
I could do this, and that with no rash potion,
But with a lingering dram that should not work   320
Maliciously like poison. But I cannot
Believe this crack to be in my dread mistress,   322
So sovereignly being honorable.
I have loved thee –   324

LEONTES   Make that thy question, and go rot!
Dost think I am so muddy, so unsettled,
To appoint myself in this vexation, sully   326
The purity and whiteness of my sheets –
Which to preserve is sleep, which being spotted

---

302 *hovering* irresolute **306** *glass* hourglass **309** *bare* bore, had **313** *meaner form* humbler position **314** *benched* placed in authority; *worship* position of honor **322** *crack* flaw; *dread* revered **324** (since Camillo would not normally use the familiar "thee" in addressing his king, some editors assign this entire line to Leontes) **326** *appoint . . . vexation* work myself into this frenzy

Is goads, thorns, nettles, tails of wasps –
330   Give scandal to the blood o' th' prince my son,
Who I do think is mine and love as mine,
332   Without ripe moving to't? Would I do this?
333   Could man so blench?

CAMILLO   I must believe you, sir.
I do, and will fetch off Bohemia for't;
Provided that, when he's removed, your highness
Will take again your queen as yours at first,
Even for your son's sake, and thereby for sealing
The injury of tongues in courts and kingdoms
Known and allied to yours.

LEONTES   Thou dost advise me
340   Even so as I mine own course have set down.
I'll give no blemish to her honor, none.

CAMILLO   My lord,
Go then, and with a countenance as clear
As friendship wears at feasts, keep with Bohemia
And with your queen. I am his cupbearer.
If from me he have wholesome beverage,
Account me not your servant.

LEONTES   This is all.
Do't, and thou hast the one half of my heart;
Do't not, thou split'st thine own.

CAMILLO   I'll do't, my lord.

LEONTES
I will seem friendly, as thou hast advised me.   *Exit.*

CAMILLO
350   O miserable lady! But for me,
What case stand I in? I must be the poisoner
Of good Polixenes; and my ground to do't
Is the obedience to a master, one
Who in rebellion with himself will have
All that are his so too. To do this deed,
Promotion follows. If I could find example

---

332 *ripe moving* good reason   333 *blench* deceive himself

Of thousands that had struck anointed kings
And flourished after, I'd not do't; but since
Nor brass nor stone nor parchment bears not one,
Let villainy itself forswear't. I must   *360*
Forsake the court. To do't, or no, is certain   *361*
To me a break-neck. Happy star reign now!   *362*
Here comes Bohemia.
        Enter Polixenes.
POLIXENES   This is strange. Methinks
My favor here begins to warp. Not speak?   *364*
Good day, Camillo.
CAMILLO   Hail, most royal sir!
POLIXENES
What is the news i' th' court?   *366*
CAMILLO   None rare, my lord.
POLIXENES
The king hath on him such a countenance
As he had lost some province and a region
Loved as he loves himself. Even now I met him   *369*
With customary compliment, when he,   *370*
Wafting his eyes to th' contrary and falling
A lip of much contempt, speeds from me, and
So leaves me to consider what is breeding
That changes thus his manners.
CAMILLO
I dare not know, my lord.
POLIXENES
How dare not? do not? Do you know and dare not?
Be intelligent to me. 'Tis thereabouts,   *377*
For, to yourself, what you do know, you must,
And cannot say you dare not. Good Camillo,
Your changed complexions are to me a mirror   *380*

---

361 *To do't* to kill Polixenes   362 *To . . . break-neck* death to me; *Happy star*
good fortune   364 *Not speak* (Polixenes refers to Leontes, whom he encoun-
tered on his way in)   366 *rare* unusual   369 *met* greeted   377 *intelligent* in-
telligible; *'Tis thereabouts* it is something of the sort

    Which shows me mine changed too, for I must be
    A party in this alteration, finding
    Myself thus altered with't.
CAMILLO   There is a sickness
    Which puts some of us in distemper, but
    I cannot name the disease, and it is caught
    Of you that yet are well.
POLIXENES   How caught of me?
387   Make me not sighted like the basilisk.
    I have looked on thousands who have sped the better
389   By my regard, but killed none so. Camillo,
390   As you are certainly a gentleman, thereto
391   Clerklike experienced – which no less adorns
    Our gentry than our parents' noble names,
393   In whose success we are gentle – I beseech you,
394   If you know aught which does behove my knowledge
    Thereof to be informed, imprison't not
    In ignorant concealment.
CAMILLO   I may not answer.
POLIXENES
    A sickness caught of me, and yet I well?
    I must be answered. Dost thou hear, Camillo?
399   I conjure thee by all the parts of man
400   Which honor does acknowledge, whereof the least
    Is not this suit of mine, that thou declare
402   What incidency thou dost guess of harm
    Is creeping toward me; how far off, how near;
    Which way to be prevented, if to be;
    If not, how best to bear it.
CAMILLO   Sir, I will tell you,
    Since I am charged in honor and by him
    That I think honorable. Therefore mark my counsel,

---

387 *Make . . . basilisk* attribute not to me a sight like that of the fabulous serpent whose look or breath was fatal **389** *regard* look **391** *Clerklike* like a scholar **393** *In whose success* in succession from whom **394–95** *does . . . informed* I need to know **399** *parts* duties **402** *incidency* happening

Which must be even as swiftly followed as
I mean to utter it, or both yourself and me
Cry "Lost," and so good night!   410

POLIXENES   On, good Camillo.

CAMILLO
I am appointed him to murder you.

POLIXENES
By whom, Camillo?

CAMILLO   By the king.

POLIXENES   For what?

CAMILLO
He thinks, nay, with all confidence he swears,
As he had seen't or been an instrument
To vice you to't, that you have touched his queen   415
Forbiddenly.

POLIXENES   O, then my best blood turn
To an infected jelly and my name
Be yoked with his that did betray the Best!   418
Turn then my freshest reputation to
A savor that may strike the dullest nostril   420
Where I arrive, and my approach be shunned,
Nay, hated too, worse than the great'st infection
That e'er was heard or read!

CAMILLO   Swear his thought over
By each particular star in heaven and
By all their influences, you may as well
Forbid the sea for to obey the moon
As or by oath remove or counsel shake   427
The fabric of his folly, whose foundation
Is piled upon his faith and will continue
The standing of his body.   430

POLIXENES   How should this grow?

CAMILLO
I know not. But I am sure 'tis safer to

---

410 *good night* this is the end (an expression of finality) **415** *vice* force
418 *Best* Jesus (betrayed by Judas) **427** *or . . . or* either . . . or

Avoid what's grown than question how 'tis born.
If therefore you dare trust my honesty,
434   That lies enclosèd in this trunk which you
435   Shall bear along impawned, away tonight!
436   Your followers I will whisper to the business,
437   And will by twos and threes at several posterns
Clear them o' th' city. For myself, I'll put
My fortunes to your service, which are here
440   By this discovery lost. Be not uncertain,
For, by the honor of my parents, I
Have uttered truth, which if you seek to prove,
I dare not stand by; nor shall you be safer
Than one condemned by the king's own mouth,
Thereon his execution sworn.
POLIXENES   I do believe thee;
I saw his heart in's face. Give me thy hand.
447   Be pilot to me and thy places shall
Still neighbor mine. My ships are ready and
My people did expect my hence departure
450   Two days ago. This jealousy
Is for a precious creature. As she's rare,
Must it be great; and as his person's mighty,
Must it be violent; and as he does conceive
He is dishonored by a man which ever
455   Professed to him, why, his revenges must
456   In that be made more bitter. Fear o'ershades me.
457   Good expedition be my friend, and comfort
458   The gracious queen, part of his theme but nothing
Of his ill-ta'en suspicion! Come, Camillo.
460   I will respect thee as a father if
461   Thou bear'st my life off, hence: let us avoid.

---

434 *trunk* body   435 *impawned* as a pledge   436 *whisper to* secretly tell of
437 *posterns* back doors   447–48 *thy places . . . mine* i.e., I'll always keep you
near me   455 *Professed* professed love   456 *o'ershades* covers   457 *expedition* prompt action   458–59 *part . . . suspicion* also object of the king's anger
though innocent of wrongdoing   461 *avoid* depart

CAMILLO
   It is in mine authority to command
   The keys of all the posterns. Please your highness
   To take the urgent hour. Come, sir, away.   *Exeunt.*

                    ✳

∽ **II.1** *Enter Hermione, Mamillius, Ladies.*

HERMIONE
   Take the boy to you. He so troubles me,   1
   'Tis past enduring.
LADY   Come, my gracious lord,
   Shall I be your playfellow?
MAMILLIUS   No, I'll none of you.
LADY
   Why, my sweet lord?
MAMILLIUS
   You'll kiss me hard and speak to me as if
   I were a baby still. I love you better.
SECOND LADY
   And why so, my lord?
MAMILLIUS   Not for because
   Your brows are blacker. Yet black brows, they say,   8
   Become some women best, so that there be not
   Too much hair there, but in a semicircle,   *10*
   Or a half-moon made with a pen.   *11*
SECOND LADY   Who taught this?
MAMILLIUS
   I learned it out of women's faces. Pray now,
   What color are your eyebrows?
LADY   Blue, my lord.
MAMILLIUS
   Nay, that's a mock. I have seen a lady's nose
   That has been blue, but not her eyebrows.

II.1 In Leontes' palace   **1** *Take . . . you* take charge of the boy   **8** *blacker* (1)
darker, (2) less "fair" or beautiful   **11** *taught'* taught thee

LADY   Hark ye.
16   The queen your mother rounds apace. We shall
      Present our services to a fine new prince
18   One of these days, and then you'd wanton with us,
      If we would have you.
SECOND LADY   She is spread of late
20   Into a goodly bulk. Good time encounter her!
HERMIONE
21   What wisdom stirs amongst you? Come, sir, now
      I am for you again. Pray you sit by us
      And tell's a tale.
MAMILLIUS   Merry or sad shall't be?
HERMIONE
      As merry as you will.
MAMILLIUS
      A sad tale's best for winter. I have one
      Of sprites and goblins.
HERMIONE   Let's have that, good sir.
      Come on, sit down. Come on, and do your best
      To fright me with your sprites; you're powerful at it.
MAMILLIUS
      There was a man –
HERMIONE   Nay, come sit down; then on.
MAMILLIUS
30   Dwelt by a churchyard. I will tell it softly;
31   Yond crickets shall not hear it.
HERMIONE   Come on, then,
      And give't me in mine ear.
          [Enter] Leontes, Antigonus, Lords [, and others].
LEONTES
      Was he met there? his train? Camillo with him?
LORD
      Behind the tuft of pines I met them. Never

---

16 *rounds apace* rapidly grows rounder   18 *wanton* play   20 *Good time encounter* good fortune attend   21 *wisdom stirs* wise matter is discussed   31 *crickets* i.e., the ladies-in-waiting, who may be talking or laughing

Saw I men scour so on their way. I eyed them   35
Even to their ships.
LEONTES   How blest am I
In my just censure, in my true opinion!
Alack, for lesser knowledge! how accursed   38
In being so blest! There may be in the cup
A spider steeped, and one may drink, depart,   40
And yet partake no venom, for his knowledge
Is not infected; but if one present
Th' abhorred ingredient to his eye, make known
How he hath drunk, he cracks his gorge, his sides,
With violent hefts. I have drunk, and seen the spider.   45
Camillo was his help in this, his pander.
There is a plot against my life, my crown.
All's true that is mistrusted. That false villain   48
Whom I employed was preemployed by him.
He has discovered my design, and I   50
Remain a pinched thing – yea, a very trick   51
For them to play at will. How came the posterns
So easily open?
LORD   By his great authority,
Which often hath no less prevailed than so
On your command.
LEONTES   I know't too well.
Give me the boy. I am glad you did not nurse him.
Though he does bear some signs of me, yet you
Have too much blood in him.   58
HERMIONE   What is this? sport?
LEONTES
Bear the boy hence. He shall not come about her.
Away with him! and let her sport herself   60
With that she's big with, for 'tis Polixenes
Has made thee swell thus.

---

35 *scour* hasten 38 *Alack . . . knowledge* O, that my knowledge were less
45 *hefts* heavings 48 *mistrusted* suspected 50 *discovered* revealed 51
pinched tortured; *trick* toy 58 *sport* jesting

HERMIONE   But I'd say he had not,
And I'll be sworn you would believe my saying,
64   Howe'er you lean to the nayward.
LEONTES   You, my lords,
Look on her, mark her well. Be but about
To say "She is a goodly lady," and
The justice of your hearts will thereto add
"'Tis pity she's not honest, honorable."
69   Praise her but for this her without-door form –
70   Which on my faith deserves high speech – and straight
71   The shrug, the hum or ha, these petty brands
72   That calumny doth use – O, I am out,
73   That mercy does, for calumny will sear
Virtue itself – these shrugs, these hums and ha's,
75   When you have said she's goodly, come between
Ere you can say she's honest. But be't known,
From him that has most cause to grieve it should be,
She's an adulteress.
HERMIONE   Should a villain say so,
79   The most replenished villain in the world,
80   He were as much more villain. You, my lord,
Do but mistake.
LEONTES   You have mistook, my lady,
Polixenes for Leontes. O thou thing!
83   Which I'll not call a creature of thy place,
Lest barbarism, making me the precedent,
Should a like language use to all degrees
And mannerly distinguishment leave out
Betwixt the prince and beggar. I have said
She's an adulteress; I have said with whom.
More, she's a traitor and Camillo is
90   A federary with her, and one that knows

---

64 *nayward* negative   69 *without-door form* outward appearance   70 *straight* immediately   71 *brands* stigmas   72 *calumny* slander; *out* mistaken 72–76 (while slander will denounce even the virtuous, these "hums and ha's" are not slanderous but rather merciful, since they seek to shield Hermione from deserved reproach)   73 *sear* wither, stigmatize   75 *come between* interfere   79 *replenished* complete   83 *place* rank   90 *federary* confederate

What she should shame to know herself
But with her most vile principal, that she's
A bed-swerver, even as bad as those　　　　　　　　　93
That vulgars give bold'st titles – ay, and privy　　94
To this their late escape.

HERMIONE　　　　　　　No, by my life,
Privy to none of this. How will this grieve you,
When you shall come to clearer knowledge, that
You thus have published me! Gentle my lord,　　98
You scarce can right me throughly then to say　99
You did mistake.

LEONTES　　　　　　No. If I mistake
In those foundations which I build upon,
The center is not big enough to bear　　　　　　102
A schoolboy's top. Away with her to prison!
He who shall speak for her is afar off guilty　　104
But that he speaks.

HERMIONE　　　　　There's some ill planet reigns.
I must be patient till the heavens look
With an aspect more favorable. Good my lords,
I am not prone to weeping, as our sex
Commonly are; the want of which vain dew
Perchance shall dry your pities. But I have　　　110
That honorable grief lodged here which burns
Worse than tears drown. Beseech you all, my lords,
With thoughts so qualified as your charities　　113
Shall best instruct you, measure me; and so　　114
The king's will be performed.

LEONTES　　　　　　　Shall I be heard?

HERMIONE
Who is't that goes with me? Beseech your highness,
My women may be with me, for you see
My plight requires it. Do not weep, good fools;　　118

---

93 *bed-swerver* adulterer　94 *vulgars . . . titles* common people call rudest names　98 *published* made a public spectacle of　99 *throughly* thoroughly; *then* except　102 *center* earth　104–5 *He . . . speaks* he is indirectly guilty who merely speaks in her behalf　113 *qualified* modified　114 *measure* judge　118 *fools* (a term of endearment)

There is no cause. When you shall know your mistress
120 Has deserved prison, then abound in tears
As I come out. This action I now go on
Is for my better grace. Adieu, my lord.
I never wished to see you sorry; now
I trust I shall. My women, come; you have leave.

LEONTES
Go, do our bidding. Hence!
[Exit Queen, guarded, with Ladies.]

LORD
Beseech your highness, call the queen again.

ANTIGONUS
Be certain what you do, sir, lest your justice
Prove violence, in the which three great ones suffer,
Yourself, your queen, your son.

LORD   For her, my lord,
130 I dare my life lay down and will do't, sir,
Please you t' accept it, that the queen is spotless
I' th' eyes of heaven and to you – I mean,
In this which you accuse her.

ANTIGONUS   If it prove
134 She's otherwise, I'll keep my stables where
I lodge my wife. I'll go in couples with her,
Than when I feel and see her no farther trust her;
For every inch of woman in the world,
138 Ay, every dram of woman's flesh is false,
If she be.

LEONTES   Hold your peaces.

LORD   Good my lord –

ANTIGONUS
140 It is for you we speak, not for ourselves.
141 You are abused and by some putter-on
That will be damned for't. Would I knew the villain,

134–35 *I'll . . . her* (1) I'll run my house the way I run my stables, with the
mares kept separate from the stallions, (2) I'll guard my wife as closely as I
guard my horses   138 *dram* little bit   141 *putter-on* instigator

I would land-damn him. Be she honor-flawed,   143
I have three daughters – the eldest is eleven,
The second and the third, nine and some five –
If this prove true, they'll pay for't. By mine honor,
I'll geld 'em all; fourteen they shall not see   147
To bring false generations. They are co-heirs,   148
And I had rather glib myself than they   149
Should not produce fair issue.   *150*
LEONTES   Cease; no more.
You smell this business with a sense as cold
As is a dead man's nose; but I do see't and feel't,
As you feel doing thus *[Pinches Antigonus.]*, and see
    withal
The instruments that feel.   154
ANTIGONUS   If it be so,
We need no grave to bury honesty;
There's not a grain of it the face to sweeten
Of the whole dungy earth.   157
LEONTES   What? Lack I credit?
LORD
I had rather you did lack than I, my lord,
Upon this ground; and more it would content me   159
To have her honor true than your suspicion,   *160*
Be blamed for't how you might.
LEONTES   Why, what need we
Commune with you of this, but rather follow
Our forceful instigation? Our prerogative   163
Calls not your counsels, but our natural goodness   164
Imparts this, which if you – or stupefied   165
Or seeming so in skill – cannot or will not   166
Relish a truth like us, inform yourselves
We need no more of your advice. The matter,

---

143 *land-damn* (unclear etymology and meaning; may mean "thrash")   147
geld sterilize, "fix"   148 *bring . . . generations* bear illegitimate children   149
glib castrate   154 *instruments that feel* i.e., Leontes' fingers   157 *dungy*
soiled (by excrement); *credit* credibility   159 *ground* matter   163 *instigation*
incentive   164 *Calls* calls for   165 *Imparts* bestows   166 *skill* discernment

The loss, the gain, the ordering on't, is all
170   Properly ours.
ANTIGONUS   And I wish, my liege,
    You had only in your silent judgment tried it,
172   Without more overture.
LEONTES   How could that be?
    Either thou art most ignorant by age
    Or thou wert born a fool. Camillo's flight,
    Added to their familiarity –
    Which was as gross as ever touched conjecture,
    That lacked sight only, nought for approbation
    But only seeing, all other circumstances
    Made up to th' deed – doth push on this proceeding.
180   Yet, for a greater confirmation –
    For in an act of this importance 'twere
182   Most piteous to be wild – I have dispatched in post
183   To sacred Delphos, to Apollo's temple,
    Cleomenes and Dion, whom you know
185   Of stuffed sufficiency. Now from the oracle
    They will bring all, whose spiritual counsel had,
    Shall stop or spur me. Have I done well?
LORD
    Well done, my lord.
LEONTES
    Though I am satisfied and need no more
190   Than what I know, yet shall the oracle
    Give rest to th' minds of others, such as he
    Whose ignorant credulity will not
193   Come up to th' truth. So have we thought it good
194   From our free person she should be confined,
    Lest that the treachery of the two fled hence

---

172 *overture* public revelation   182 *wild* rash; *post* haste   183 *sacred Delphos . . . Apollo's temple* (Delos, the Greek island thought to be the god Apollo's birthplace, was often known as Delphos in the Renaissance. Here, as elsewhere in the period, it is conflated with Delphi, a sacred place on the mainland where the oracle of Apollo, a priest through whom the god supposedly spoke, could be consulted.)   185 *stuffed sufficiency* full competence   193 *Come up to* face   194 *free* easily accessible

Be left her to perform. Come, follow us.
We are to speak in public, for this business
Will raise us all.   198
ANTIGONUS   *[Aside]* To laughter, as I take it,
If the good truth were known.   *Exeunt.*

                              *

∾ **II.2** *Enter Paulina, a Gentleman [, and Attendants].*

PAULINA
The keeper of the prison, call to him;
Let him have knowledge who I am.   *[Exit Gentleman.]*
                                        Good lady,
No court in Europe is too good for thee.
What dost thou then in prison?
    [Enter Gentleman with the] Jailer.
                                        Now, good sir,
You know me, do you not?
JAILER   For a worthy lady
And one who much I honor.
PAULINA   Pray you then,
Conduct me to the queen.
JAILER   I may not, madam.
To the contrary I have express commandment.
PAULINA
Here's ado,
To lock up honesty and honor from   *10*
Th' access of gentle visitors. Is't lawful, pray you,   11
To see her women? any of them? Emilia?
JAILER
So please you, madam,
To put apart these your attendants, I
Shall bring Emilia forth.
PAULINA   I pray now, call her.
Withdraw yourselves.

---

198 *raise* rouse
   II.2 A prison   **11** *lawful* permitted (satirical)

[Exeunt Gentleman and Attendants.]

JAILER   And, madam,
    I must be present at your conference.

PAULINA
    Well, be't so, prithee.   *[Exit Jailer.]*
    Here's such ado to make no stain a stain
20   As passes coloring.
            [Enter Jailer with] Emilia.
                              Dear gentlewoman,
    How fares our gracious lady?

EMILIA
    As well as one so great and so forlorn
    May hold together. On her frights and griefs,
    Which never tender lady hath borne greater,
25   She is something before her time delivered.

PAULINA
    A boy?

EMILIA   A daughter, and a goodly babe,
    Lusty and like to live. The queen receives
    Much comfort in't, says, "My poor prisoner,
    I am innocent as you."

PAULINA   I dare be sworn.
30   These dangerous unsafe lunes i' th' king, beshrew them!
    He must be told on't, and he shall. The office
    Becomes a woman best; I'll take't upon me.
    If I prove honey-mouthed, let my tongue blister
34   And never to my red-looked anger be
    The trumpet any more. Pray you, Emilia,
    Commend my best obedience to the queen.
    If she dares trust me with her little babe,
    I'll show't the king and undertake to be
    Her advocate to th' loud'st. We do not know
40   How he may soften at the sight o' th' child.
    The silence often of pure innocence
    Persuades when speaking fails.

---

20 *passes coloring* surpasses belief **25** *something* somewhat **30** *lunes* fits of
lunacy; *beshrew* curse **34** *red-looked* red-faced

EMILIA   Most worthy madam,
    Your honor and your goodness is so evident
    That your free undertaking cannot miss   44
    A thriving issue. There is no lady living
    So meet for this great errand. Please your ladyship
    To visit the next room, I'll presently   47
    Acquaint the queen of your most noble offer,
    Who but today hammered of this design,   49
    But durst not tempt a minister of honor   50
    Lest she should be denied.
PAULINA   Tell her, Emilia,
    I'll use that tongue I have. If wit flow from't
    As boldness from my bosom, let't not be doubted
    I shall do good.
EMILIA   Now be you blest for it!
    I'll to the queen. Please you, come something nearer.
JAILER
    Madam, if't please the queen to send the babe,
    I know not what I shall incur to pass it,
    Having no warrant.
PAULINA   You need not fear it, sir.
    This child was prisoner to the womb and is
    By law and process of great nature thence   60
    Freed and enfranchised, not a party to
    The anger of the king nor guilty of,
    If any be, the trespass of the queen.
JAILER
    I do believe it.
PAULINA
    Do not you fear. Upon mine honor, I
    Will stand betwixt you and danger.   *Exeunt.*

              *

---

44 *free* voluntary   47 *presently* at once   49 *hammered of* formulated   50
tempt try to win over

❧ **II.3** *Enter Leontes, Servants, Antigonus, and Lords.*

LEONTES
    Nor night nor day no rest. It is but weakness
    To bear the matter thus – mere weakness. If
3   The cause were not in being – part o' th' cause,
4   She, th' adulteress; for the harlot king
5   Is quite beyond mine arm, out of the blank
    And level of my brain, plot-proof. But she
    I can hook to me. Say that she were gone,
8   Given to the fire, a moiety of my rest
    Might come to me again. Who's there?
SERVANT   My lord.
LEONTES
10   How does the boy?
SERVANT   He took good rest tonight.
    'Tis hoped his sickness is discharged.
LEONTES
    To see his nobleness!
    Conceiving the dishonor of his mother,
    He straight declined, drooped, took it deeply,
15   Fastened and fixed the shame on't in himself,
    Threw off his spirit, his appetite, his sleep,
17   And downright languished. Leave me solely. Go
18   See how he fares.   *[Exit Servant.]*
               Fie, fie! no thought of him!
    The very thought of my revenges that way
20   Recoil upon me – in himself too mighty,
    And in his parties, his alliance. Let him be
    Until a time may serve. For present vengeance,
    Take it on her. Camillo and Polixenes
    Laugh at me, make their pastime at my sorrow.
    They should not laugh if I could reach them, nor

II.3 Leontes' palace   **3** *in being* alive   **4** *harlot* (a general insult that could apply to both men and women, this term started out as a reference to low social status and gradually accrued sexual connotations – e.g., lewd, promiscuous)   **5–6** *blank And level* target and aim   **8** *moiety* small part   **15** *on't* of it   **17** *solely* alone   **18** *him* i.e., Polixenes

    Shall she within my power.
     Enter Paulina [with a baby].

LORD   You must not enter.

PAULINA
    Nay, rather, good my lords, be second to me.   27
    Fear you his tyrannous passion more, alas,
    Than the queen's life? a gracious innocent soul,
    More free than he is jealous.   30

ANTIGONUS   That's enough.

SERVANT
    Madam, he hath not slept tonight, commanded
    None should come at him.

PAULINA   Not so hot, good sir.
    I come to bring him sleep. 'Tis such as you,
    That creep like shadows by him and do sigh
    At each his needless heavings; such as you
    Nourish the cause of his awaking. I
    Do come with words as medicinal as true,
    Honest as either, to purge him of that humor   38
    That presses him from sleep.

LEONTES   What noise there, ho?

PAULINA
    No noise, my lord, but needful conference   *40*
    About some gossips for your highness.   *41*

LEONTES   How?
    Away with that audacious lady! Antigonus,
    I charged thee that she should not come about me.
    I knew she would.

ANTIGONUS   I told her so, my lord,
    On your displeasure's peril and on mine,
    She should not visit you.

LEONTES   What, canst not rule her?

---

27 *be second to* assist   **30** *free* innocent   **38** *humor* disorder (this refers to the
theory that the body consisted of four fluids, or humors, which must be held
in balance to maintain emotional and physical health; here, unbalanced humors prevent Leontes from sleeping)   **41** *gossips* godparents, or baptismal
sponsors for a child

PAULINA
    From all dishonesty he can. In this,
    Unless he take the course that you have done,
49   Commit me for committing honor, trust it,
50   He shall not rule me.

ANTIGONUS   La you now, you hear!
    When she will take the rein I let her run,
    But she'll not stumble.

PAULINA   Good my liege, I come –
    And I beseech you hear me, who professes
    Myself your loyal servant, your physician,
    Your most obedient counselor, yet that dares
56   Less appear so in comforting your evils
    Than such as most seem yours – I say I come
    From your good queen.

LEONTES   Good queen?

PAULINA   Good queen, my lord,
    Good queen. I say good queen,
60   And would by combat make her good, so were I
    A man, the worst about you.

LEONTES   Force her hence.

PAULINA
    Let him that makes but trifles of his eyes
    First hand me. On mine own accord I'll off,
    But first I'll do my errand. The good queen,
    For she is good, hath brought you forth a daughter –
    Here 'tis – commends it to your blessing.
     [Lays down the child.]

LEONTES   Out!
67   A mankind witch! Hence with her, out o' door!
68   A most intelligencing bawd.

---

49 *Commit* imprison 56 *comforting* condoning 60 *by combat . . . good* I
would fight to prove her innocent (refers to a medieval method of determin-
ing guilt or innocence by either undergoing an ordeal or fighting a duel) 67
mankind masculine (Although those accused as witches were usually women,
their crime was, in part, that they acted in a decidedly unfeminine way – they
were assertive, garrulous, vindictive. Thus, paradoxically, witches were both
typically female and disturbingly "mannish." Throughout this scene, Leontes
accuses Paulina of inappropriately seizing masculine prerogatives, such as authoritative speech, from her husband and her king.) 68 *intelligencing* spying

PAULINA   Not so.
  I am as ignorant in that as you
  In so entitling me – and no less honest   70
  Than you are mad, which is enough, I'll warrant,
  As this world goes, to pass for honest.
LEONTES   Traitors!
  Will you not push her out? Give her the bastard.
  Thou dotard, thou art woman-tired, unroosted   74
  By thy dame Partlet here. Take up the bastard.   75
  Take't up, I say. Give't to thy crone.
PAULINA   Forever
  Unvenerable be thy hands, if thou
  Tak'st up the princess by that forcèd baseness   78
  Which he has put upon't!
LEONTES   He dreads his wife.
PAULINA
  So I would you did. Then 'twere past all doubt   80
  You'd call your children yours.
LEONTES   A nest of traitors!
ANTIGONUS
  I am none, by this good light.
PAULINA   Nor I, nor any
  But one that's here, and that's himself; for he
  The sacred honor of himself, his queen's,
  His hopeful son's, his babe's, betrays to slander,
  Whose sting is sharper than the sword's; and will not –
  For, as the case now stands, it is a curse
  He cannot be compelled to't – once remove
  The root of his opinion, which is rotten
  As ever oak or stone was sound.   90
LEONTES   A callet
  Of boundless tongue, who late hath beat her husband

---

74 *dotard* imbecile (of Antigonus); *woman-tired* (1) henpecked, (2) dressed
or attired by or like a woman; *unroosted* driven from the roost, homeless and
without authority   75 *Partlet* Pertelote (the hen in Chaucer's "Nun's Priest's
Tale," whose dominance of her husband almost destroyed him)   78 *forcèd
baseness* false designation as bastard   90 *callet* scold

And now baits me! This brat is none of mine;
It is the issue of Polixenes.
Hence with it, and together with the dam
Commit them to the fire!

PAULINA   It is yours,
And, might we lay th' old proverb to your charge,
So like you 'tis the worse. Behold, my lords.
Although the print be little, the whole matter
And copy of the father – eye, nose, lip,
100   The trick of's frown, his forehead, nay, the valley,
101   The pretty dimples of his chin and cheek, his smiles,
The very mold and frame of hand, nail, finger.
And thou, good goddess Nature, which hast made it
104   So like to him that got it, if thou hast
The ordering of the mind too, 'mongst all colors
106   No yellow in't, lest she suspect, as he does,
107   Her children not her husband's!

LEONTES   A gross hag!
108   And, lozel, thou art worthy to be hanged
That wilt not stay her tongue.

ANTIGONUS   Hang all the husbands
110   That cannot do that feat, you'll leave yourself
Hardly one subject.

LEONTES   Once more, take her hence!

PAULINA
A most unworthy and unnatural lord
Can do no more.

LEONTES   I'll ha' thee burnt.

PAULINA   I care not.
It is an heretic that makes the fire,
Not she which burns in't. I'll not call you tyrant;
But this most cruel usage of your queen,

---

100 *valley* cleft in chin or upper lip   101 *his* the female baby's   104 *got*
begot   106 *yellow* (traditionally the color of jealousy)   107 (in her rage,
Paulina forgets that jealousy would not lead a wife to doubt the paternity of
her children; yet Leontes' doubts are as illogical as those of a wife who would
think that her husband's infidelity casts doubt on the legitimacy of her own
children)   108 *lozel* worthless person

Not able to produce more accusation
Than your own weak-hinged fancy, something savors
Of tyranny and will ignoble make you,
Yea, scandalous to the world.   *120*

LEONTES   On your allegiance,
Out of the chamber with her! Were I a tyrant,
Where were her life? She durst not call me so
If she did know me one. Away with her!

PAULINA
I pray you do not push me; I'll be gone.
Look to your babe, my lord; 'tis yours. Jove send her
A better guiding spirit. What needs these hands?   *126*
You that are thus so tender o'er his follies
Will never do him good, not one of you.
So, so. Farewell; we are gone.   *Exit.*

LEONTES
Thou, traitor, hast set on thy wife to this.   *130*
My child? away with't! Even thou, that hast
A heart so tender o'er it, take it hence
And see it instantly consumed with fire –
Even thou and none but thou. Take it up straight.
Within this hour bring me word 'tis done,
And by good testimony, or I'll seize thy life,
With what thou else call'st thine. If thou refuse
And wilt encounter with my wrath, say so.
The bastard brains with these my proper hands   *139*
Shall I dash out. Go, take it to the fire,   *140*
For thou set'st on thy wife.

ANTIGONUS   I did not, sir.
These lords, my noble fellows, if they please,
Can clear me in't.

LORDS   We can. My royal liege,
He is not guilty of her coming hither.

LEONTES
You're liars all.

---

126 *these hands* i.e., those that push her   **130** *Thou* i.e., Antigonus   **139**
proper own

LORD
Beseech your highness, give us better credit.
147 We have always truly served you, and beseech'
So to esteem of us; and on our knees we beg,
As recompense of our dear services
150 Past and to come, that you do change this purpose,
Which being so horrible, so bloody, must
Lead on to some foul issue. We all kneel.

LEONTES
I am a feather for each wind that blows.
Shall I live on to see this bastard kneel
And call me father? Better burn it now
156 Than curse it then. But be it; let it live.
157 It shall not neither. You, sir, come you hither,
You that have been so tenderly officious
159 With Lady Margery, your midwife there,
160 To save this bastard's life – for 'tis a bastard,
So sure as this beard's gray. What will you adventure
To save this brat's life?

ANTIGONUS   Anything, my lord,
163 That my ability may undergo
And nobleness impose. At least thus much.
165 I'll pawn the little blood which I have left
To save the innocent. Anything possible.

LEONTES
It shall be possible. Swear by this sword
Thou wilt perform my bidding.

ANTIGONUS   I will, my lord.

LEONTES
169 Mark and perform it, seest thou; for the fail
170 Of any point in't shall not only be
Death to thyself but to thy lewd-tongued wife,
Whom for this time we pardon. We enjoin thee,

---

147 *beseech'* (with "you" understood)   156 *be it* so be it   157 *It . . . neither*
it still won't be able to call me father   159 *Margery* (a contemptuous term
for an uppity woman; "margery-prater" was a slang term for a hen)   163 *undergo* perform   165 *pawn* pledge   169 *fail* failure

As thou art liege man to us, that thou carry
This female bastard hence, and that thou bear it
To some remote and desert place quite out
Of our dominions, and that there thou leave it,
Without more mercy, to it own protection   177
And favor of the climate. As by strange fortune   178
It came to us, I do in justice charge thee,
On thy soul's peril and thy body's torture,   180
That thou commend it strangely to some place   181
Where chance may nurse or end it. Take it up.

ANTIGONUS
I swear to do this, though a present death
Had been more merciful. Come on, poor babe.
Some powerful spirit instruct the kites and ravens   185
To be thy nurses. Wolves and bears, they say,
Casting their savageness aside, have done
Like offices of pity. Sir, be prosperous
In more than this deed does require. And blessing   189
Against this cruelty fight on thy side,   190
Poor thing, condemned to loss.   *Exit [with the baby].*

LEONTES   No, I'll not rear
Another's issue.
      Enter a Servant.

SERVANT   Please your highness, posts
From those you sent to th' oracle are come
An hour since. Cleomenes and Dion,
Being well arrived from Delphos, are both landed,
Hasting to th' court.

LORD   So please you, sir, their speed
Hath been beyond account.   197

LEONTES   Twenty-three days
They have been absent. 'Tis good speed, foretells
The great Apollo suddenly will have   199

---

177 *it* its   178 *strange* (1) unusual, mysterious, (2) foreign (Polixenes, whom
he declares the father and estranges from himself as a foreigner rather than a
"brother")   181 *commend . . . place* commit it to some foreign place   185
kites birds of prey   189 *require* deserve   197 *account* record   199 *suddenly*
at once

200   The truth of this appear. Prepare you, lords;
201   Summon a session, that we may arraign
        Our most disloyal lady, for, as she hath
        Been publicly accused, so shall she have
        A just and open trial. While she lives
        My heart will be a burden to me. Leave me,
        And think upon my bidding.   *Exeunt.*

*

❧ **III.1** *Enter Cleomenes and Dion.*

CLEOMENES
    The climate's delicate, the air most sweet,
    Fertile the isle, the temple much surpassing
    The common praise it bears.

DION   I shall report,
4   For most it caught me, the celestial habits –
        Methinks I so should term them – and the reverence
        Of the grave wearers. O, the sacrifice,
        How ceremonious, solemn, and unearthly
8   It was i' th' offering!

CLEOMENES   But of all, the burst
    And the ear-deafening voice o' th' oracle,
10   Kin to Jove's thunder, so surprised my sense
11   That I was nothing.

DION   If th' event o' th' journey
    Prove as successful to the queen – O be't so! –
    As it hath been to us rare, pleasant, speedy,
14   The time is worth the use on't.

CLEOMENES   Great Apollo
    Turn all to th' best! These proclamations,
    So forcing faults upon Hermione,
    I little like.

---

201 *session* (of the court), a trial
    III.1 Somewhere on the journey back to Sicilia   **4** *caught* struck; *habits*
costumes   **8** *burst* blast (of thunder)   **11** *nothing* overwhelmed, stunned;
event outcome   **14** *worth . . . on't* well spent

DION   The violent carriage of it
  Will clear or end the business. When the oracle,
  Thus by Apollo's great divine sealed up,
  Shall the contents discover, something rare   *20*
  Even then will rush to knowledge. Go. Fresh horses!
  And gracious be the issue!   *Exeunt.* *22*

                          ✳

∾ **III.2** *Enter Leontes, Lords, Officers.*

LEONTES
  This sessions, to our great grief we pronounce,
  Even pushes 'gainst our heart – the party tried
  The daughter of a king, our wife, and one
  Of us too much beloved. Let us be cleared   *4*
  Of being tyrannous, since we so openly
  Proceed in justice, which shall have due course,
  Even to the guilt or the purgation.   *7*
  Produce the prisoner.
OFFICER
  It is his highness' pleasure that the queen
  Appear in person here in court. Silence!   *10*
      [Enter] Hermione, as to her trial, [Paulina, and] Ladies.
LEONTES
  Read the indictment.
OFFICER *[Reads.]* Hermione, queen to the worthy Leontes,
  king of Sicilia, thou art here accused and arraigned of
  high treason, in committing adultery with Polixenes, *14*
  king of Bohemia, and conspiring with Camillo to take
  away the life of our sovereign lord the king, thy royal
  husband; the pretense whereof being by circumstances *17*
  partly laid open, thou, Hermione, contrary to the faith

---

22 *issue* result
  III.2 A court of justice in Sicilia 4 *Of* by 7 *purgation* clearing 14
  (Leontes construes adultery as high treason both because it would cast doubt
  on the succession and because it would motivate the queen to conspire
  against her husband's life) 17 *pretense* purpose

and allegiance of a true subject, didst counsel and aid
20   them, for their better safety, to fly away by night.
HERMIONE
    Since what I am to say must be but that
    Which contradicts my accusation, and
    The testimony on my part no other
24   But what comes from myself, it shall scarce boot me
    To say, "Not guilty." Mine integrity,
    Being counted falsehood, shall, as I express it,
    Be so received. But thus: if powers divine
    Behold our human actions, as they do,
    I doubt not then but innocence shall make
30   False accusation blush and tyranny
    Tremble at patience. You, my lord, best know,
    Who least will seem to do so, my past life
    Hath been as continent, as chaste, as true,
    As I am now unhappy; which is more
35   Than history can pattern, though devised
36   And played to take spectators. For behold me –
37   A fellow of the royal bed, which owe
38   A moiety of the throne, a great king's daughter,
    The mother to a hopeful prince – here standing
40   To prate and talk for life and honor 'fore
41   Who please to come and hear. For life, I prize it
    As I weigh grief, which I would spare. For honor,
43   'Tis a derivative from me to mine,
    And only that I stand for. I appeal
    To your own conscience, sir, before Polixenes
    Came to your court, how I was in your grace,
    How merited to be so; since he came,
48   With what encounter so uncurrent I
49   Have strained t' appear thus; if one jot beyond
50   The bound of honor, or in act or will

---

24 *boot* profit   35 *history* story, narrative; *pattern* match   36 *take* please   37 *owe* own   38 *moiety* share   41–42 (as for life, I value it as much as I value grief, which I could do without)   43 *a derivative . . . mine* something to be inherited by my children from me   48 *uncurrent* unlawful   49 *strained* sinned

That way inclining, hardened be the hearts
Of all that hear me, and my near'st of kin
Cry fie upon my grave!
LEONTES   I ne'er heard yet
That any of these bolder vices wanted
Less impudence to gainsay what they did
Than to perform it first.
HERMIONE   That's true enough,
Though 'tis a saying, sir, not due to me.   57
LEONTES
You will not own it.   58
HERMIONE   More than mistress of
Which comes to me in name of fault, I must not
At all acknowledge. For Polixenes,   60
With whom I am accused, I do confess
I loved him as in honor he required –   62
With such a kind of love as might become
A lady like me, with a love even such,
So and no other, as yourself commanded –
Which not to have done I think had been in me
Both disobedience and ingratitude
To you and toward your friend, whose love had spoke,
Even since it could speak, from an infant, freely
That it was yours. Now, for conspiracy,   70
I know not how it tastes, though it be dished
For me to try how. All I know of it
Is that Camillo was an honest man;
And why he left your court, the gods themselves,
Wotting no more than I, are ignorant.   75
LEONTES
You knew of his departure, as you know
What you have underta'en to do in's absence.

---

57 *due to me* applicable to my behavior   58–59 *More . . . fault* more faults
than I have   62 *required* deserved   70–72 *Now . . . how* I would not know
how conspiracy tastes if it were served to me   75 *Wotting* if they know

HERMIONE
  Sir,
  You speak a language that I understand not,
80 My life stands in the level of your dreams,
  Which I'll lay down.

LEONTES   Your actions are my dreams.
  You had a bastard by Polixenes,
  And I but dreamed it. As you were past all shame –
84 Those of your fact are so – so past all truth,
85 Which to deny concerns more than avails; for as
  Thy brat hath been cast out, like to itself,
  No father owning it – which is, indeed,
  More criminal in thee than it – so thou
  Shalt feel our justice, in whose easiest passage
90 Look for no less than death.

HERMIONE   Sir, spare your threats.
91 The bug which you would fright me with I seek.
92 To me can life be no commodity.
  The crown and comfort of my life, your favor,
  I do give lost, for I do feel it gone,
  But know not how it went. My second joy
  And first-fruits of my body, from his presence
  I am barred, like one infectious. My third comfort,
98 Starred most unluckily, is from my breast,
  The innocent milk in it most innocent mouth,
100 Haled out to murder. Myself on every post
101 Proclaimed a strumpet: with immodest hatred
102 The child-bed privilege denied, which 'longs
  To women of all fashion. Lastly, hurried
  Here to this place, i' th' open air, before
105 I have got strength of limit. Now, my liege,

---

80 *in* on   84 *fact* deed   85 *concerns* implicates   91 *bug* bugbear, bogeyman
92 *commodity* comfort   98 *Starred* fated   100 *Haled* dragged; *every post*
(public notices were fastened on posts)   101 *immodest* immoderate   102
child-bed privilege the customary period of recuperating from delivery   105
I . . . limit before I have reached the end of my post-delivery rest and recovery, and thereby regained my strength

Tell me what blessings I have here alive,
That I should fear to die? Therefore proceed.
But yet hear this – mistake me not, no life   108
(I prize it not a straw) but for mine honor,
Which I would free. If I shall be condemned   110
Upon surmises, all proofs sleeping else
But what your jealousies awake, I tell you
'Tis rigor and not law. Your honors all,
I do refer me to the oracle.
Apollo be my judge!
LORD   This your request
   Is altogether just. Therefore bring forth,
   And in Apollo's name, his oracle.
                              [Exeunt certain Officers.]
HERMIONE
   The emperor of Russia was my father.
   O that he were alive, and here beholding
   His daughter's trial; that he did but see   120
   The flatness of my misery – yet with eyes   121
   Of pity, not revenge.
      [Enter Officers with] Cleomenes, [and] Dion.
OFFICER
   You here shall swear upon this sword of justice,
   That you, Cleomenes and Dion, have
   Been both at Delphos, and from thence have brought
   This sealed-up oracle, by the hand delivered
   Of great Apollo's priest, and that since then
   You have not dared to break the holy seal
   Nor read the secrets in't.
CLEOMENES, DION   All this we swear.
LEONTES
   Break up the seals and read.   130
OFFICER *[Reads.]* Hermione is chaste, Polixenes blameless,
   Camillo a true subject, Leontes a jealous tyrant, his

108–9 *no life . . . honor* I speak not to beg for life but to defend my honor
121 *flatness* complete and unrelieved nature   130 *up* open

innocent babe truly begotten; and the king shall live
without an heir if that which is lost be not found.

LORDS
Now blessèd be the great Apollo!

HERMIONE   Praisèd!

LEONTES
Hast thou read truth?

OFFICER   Ay, my lord, even so
As it is here set down.

LEONTES
There is no truth at all i' th' oracle.
The sessions shall proceed. This is mere falsehood.
    [Enter Servant.]

SERVANT
140   My lord, the king, the king!

LEONTES   What is the business?

SERVANT
O sir, I shall be hated to report it.
142   The prince your son, with mere conceit and fear
143   Of the queen's speed, is gone.

LEONTES   How? gone?

SERVANT   Is dead.

LEONTES
Apollo's angry, and the heavens themselves
Do strike at my injustice.
    [Hermione swoons.]   How now there?

PAULINA
146   This news is mortal to the queen. Look down
And see what death is doing.

LEONTES   Take her hence.
148   Her heart is but o'ercharged; she will recover.
I have too much believed mine own suspicion.
150   Beseech you, tenderly apply to her
Some remedies for life.
                    [Exeunt Paulina and Ladies with Hermione.]

---

142 *conceit* imagination; *fear* anxiety   143 *speed* fortune, fate   146 *mortal*
fatal   148 *o'ercharged* too full (of grief)

                    Apollo, pardon
My great profaneness 'gainst thine oracle!
I'll reconcile me to Polixenes,
New woo my queen, recall the good Camillo,
Whom I proclaim a man of truth, of mercy;
For, being transported by my jealousies
To bloody thoughts and to revenge, I chose
Camillo for the minister to poison
My friend Polixenes, which had been done,
But that the good mind of Camillo tardied   160
My swift command, though I with death and with   161
Reward did threaten and encourage him,
Not doing it and being done. He, most humane
And filled with honor, to my kingly guest
Unclasped my practice, quit his fortunes here,   165
Which you knew great, and to the hazard
Of all incertainties himself commended,   167
No richer than his honor. How he glisters   168
Through my rust! and how his piety   169
Does my deeds make the blacker!   170
    [Enter Paulina.]

PAULINA   Woe the while!
O, cut my lace, lest my heart, cracking it,   171
Break too!

LORD   What fit is this, good lady?

PAULINA
What studied torments, tyrant, hast for me?
What wheels? racks? fires? what flaying? boiling
In leads or oils? what old or newer torture
Must I receive, whose every word deserves
To taste of thy most worst? Thy tyranny,
Together working with thy jealousies,

---

160 *tardied* held up, delayed   161–63 *I . . . done* I threatened him with
death if he didn't do it, and I encouraged him by hinting that he'd earn a reward if he did do it   165 *Unclasped my practice* revealed my evil design   167
commended entrusted   168 *glisters* shines   169 *Through* (pronounced as two
syllables)   170 *while* time   171 *lace* (a string tying together the stays in a
tight bodice)

Fancies too weak for boys, too green and idle
180 For girls of nine, O, think what they have done,
And then run mad indeed, stark mad, for all
182 Thy bygone fooleries were but spices of it.
That thou betrayedst Polixenes, 'twas nothing;
184 That did but show thee, of a fool, inconstant
And damnable ingrateful. Nor was't much
Thou wouldst have poisoned good Camillo's honor,
187 To have him kill a king – poor trespasses,
More monstrous standing by. Whereof I reckon
The casting forth to crows thy baby daughter
190 To be or none or little, though a devil
Would have shed water out of fire ere done't.
Nor is't directly laid to thee, the death
Of the young prince, whose honorable thoughts,
194 Thoughts high for one so tender, cleft the heart
That could conceive a gross and foolish sire
Blemished his gracious dam. This is not, no,
Laid to thy answer. But the last – O lords,
When I have said, cry "Woe!" – the queen, the queen,
The sweet'st dear'st creature's dead, and vengeance for't
200 Not dropped down yet.

LORD   The higher powers forbid!

PAULINA
I say she's dead; I'll swear't. If word nor oath
Prevail not, go and see. If you can bring
203 Tincture or luster in her lip, her eye,
Heat outwardly or breath within, I'll serve you
As I would do the gods. But, O thou tyrant,
Do not repent these things, for they are heavier
207 Than all thy woes can stir. Therefore betake thee
To nothing but despair. A thousand knees
Ten thousand years together, naked, fasting,
210 Upon a barren mountain, and still winter

---

182 *spices* foretastes, appetizers   184 *of a fool* for a fool   187–88 *poor . . . by*
slight sins compared to others you are guilty of   194 *tender* i.e., young   203
Tincture . . . eye color to the lip or brightness to the eye   207 *stir* alter

In storm perpetual, could not move the gods
To look that way thou wert.　　　　　　　　　　　　212
LEONTES　　　　　　　　　　Go on, go on.
　Thou canst not speak too much. I have deserved
　All tongues to talk their bitt'rest.
LORD　　　　　　　　　　　　Say no more.
　Howe'er the business goes, you have made fault
　I' th' boldness of your speech.
PAULINA　　　　　　　　　　I am sorry for't.
　All faults I make, when I shall come to know them,
　I do repent. Alas, I have showed too much
　The rashness of a woman. He is touched
　To the noble heart. What's gone and what's past help　220
　Should be past grief. Do not receive affliction
　At my petition. I beseech you, rather
　Let me be punished, that have minded you　　　　223
　Of what you should forget. Now, good my liege,
　Sir, royal sir, forgive a foolish woman.
　The love I bore your queen – lo, fool again! –
　I'll speak of her no more, nor of your children;
　I'll not remember you of my own lord,
　Who is lost too. Take your patience to you,　　　229
　And I'll say nothing.　　　　　　　　　　　　　230
LEONTES　　　　　　　Thou didst speak but well
　When most the truth, which I receive much better
　Than to be pitied of thee. Prithee, bring me
　To the dead bodies of my queen and son.
　One grave shall be for both. Upon them shall
　The causes of their death appear, unto
　Our shame perpetual. Once a day I'll visit
　The chapel where they lie, and tears shed there
　Shall be my recreation. So long as nature
　Will bear up with this exercise, so long
　I daily vow to use it. Come, and lead me　　　　240
　To these sorrows.　　　　　　　　　*Exeunt.*

---

212 *look . . . wert* take notice of you　**223** *minded* reminded　**229** *Take . . .
you* be patient

*

∽ **III.3** *Enter Antigonus, [and] a Mariner, [with a] bab[y].*

ANTIGONUS
1   Thou art perfect then our ship hath touched upon
     The deserts of Bohemia?
MARINER   Ay, my lord, and fear
     We have landed in ill time. The skies look grimly
4   And threaten present blusters. In my conscience,
5   The heavens with that we have in hand are angry
     And frown upon's.
ANTIGONUS
     Their sacred wills be done! Go, get aboard;
8   Look to thy bark. I'll not be long before
     I call upon thee.
MARINER   Make your best haste, and go not
10   Too far i' th' land. 'Tis like to be loud weather.
     Besides, this place is famous for the creatures
12   Of prey that keep upon't.
ANTIGONUS   Go thou away;
     I'll follow instantly.
MARINER   I am glad at heart
     To be so rid o' th' business.   *Exit.*
ANTIGONUS   Come, poor babe.
     I have heard, but not believed, the spirits o' th' dead
     May walk again. If such thing be, thy mother
     Appeared to me last night, for ne'er was dream
     So like a waking. To me comes a creature,
     Sometimes her head on one side, some another.
20   I never saw a vessel of like sorrow,
21   So filled and so becoming. In pure white robes,
     Like very sanctity, she did approach

III.3 The seacoast of Bohemia **1** *perfect* sure **4** *conscience* opinion
5 *that . . . hand* what we are up to **8** *bark* small boat **12** *keep* live **21**
filled brimming (with sorrow)

My cabin where I lay; thrice bowed before me,
And, gasping to begin some speech, her eyes
Became two spouts. The fury spent, anon   25
Did this break her from: "Good Antigonus,
Since fate, against thy better disposition,
Hath made thy person for the thrower-out
Of my poor babe, according to thine oath,
Places remote enough are in Bohemia;   30
There weep and leave it crying. And, for the babe
Is counted lost forever, Perdita,   32
I prithee, call't. For this ungentle business,
Put on thee by my lord, thou ne'er shalt see
Thy wife Paulina more." And so, with shrieks,
She melted into air. Affrighted much,
I did in time collect myself, and thought
This was so and no slumber. Dreams are toys;   38
Yet for this once, yea, superstitiously,
I will be squared by this. I do believe   40
Hermione hath suffered death, and that
Apollo would, this being indeed the issue   42
Of King Polixenes, it should here be laid,
Either for life or death, upon the earth
Of its right father. Blossom, speed thee well.
There lie, and there thy character; there these,   46
Which may, if fortune please, both breed thee, pretty,   47
And still rest thine. The storm begins. Poor wretch,   48
That for thy mother's fault art thus exposed
To loss and what may follow. Weep I cannot,   50
But my heart bleeds; and most accursed am I
To be by oath enjoined to this. Farewell!
The day frowns more and more. Thou'rt like to have
A lullaby too rough. I never saw
The heavens so dim by day. A savage clamor!

---

25 *anon* presently   32 *Perdita* i.e., the lost one (feminine)   38 *toys* trifles
40 *squared* ruled   42 *would* wishes   46 *character* writing; *these* i.e., gold and
the jewels by which she is later to be identified   47 *breed* rear, pay for your
upkeep   48 *rest thine* leave you with a little something

Well may I get aboard! This is the chase.
I am gone forever.   *Exit, pursued by a bear.*
　　[Enter] Shepherd.

SHEPHERD I would there were no age between ten and
three-and-twenty, or that youth would sleep out the
60　rest; for there is nothing in the between but getting
61　wenches with child, wronging the ancientry, stealing,
fighting. Hark you now. Would any but these boiled
brains of nineteen and two-and-twenty hunt this
weather? They have scared away two of my best sheep,
which I fear the wolf will sooner find than the master.
If anywhere I have them, 'tis by the seaside, browsing of
ivy. Good luck, an't be thy will! What have we here?
68　Mercy on's, a barne, a very pretty barne! A boy or a
69　child, I wonder? A pretty one, a very pretty one. Sure,
70　some scape. Though I am not bookish, yet I can read
waiting-gentlewoman in the scape. This has been some
72　stair work, some trunk work, some behind-door work.
73　They were warmer that got this than the poor thing is
here. I'll take it up for pity. Yet I'll tarry till my son
75　come. He hallooed but even now. Whoa, ho, hoa!
　　Enter Clown.

CLOWN Hilloa, loa!

SHEPHERD What, art so near? If thou'lt see a thing to
talk on when thou art dead and rotten, come hither.
What ail'st thou, man?

80 CLOWN I have seen two such sights, by sea and by land –
but I am not to say it is a sea, for it is now the sky; betwixt the firmament and it you cannot thrust a bodkin's
point.

SHEPHERD Why, boy, how is it?

CLOWN I would you did but see how it chafes, how it
rages, how it takes up the shore. But that's not to the
point. O, the most piteous cry of the poor souls! Some-

---

61 *ancientry* old people **68** *barne* baby **69** *child* girl **70** *scape* escapade
72 *trunk work* (1) done in an enclosed or secret place, (2) done with the torso
73 *got* begot **75** **s.d.** *Clown* country bumpkin

times to see 'em, and not to see 'em. Now the ship
boring the moon with her mainmast, and anon swal-   89
lowed with yest and froth, as you'd thrust a cork into a   90
hogshead. And then for the land service – to see how   91
the bear tore out his shoulder bone, how he cried to me
for help and said his name was Antigonus, a nobleman.
But to make an end of the ship – to see how the sea
flapdragoned it. But, first, how the poor souls roared,   95
and the sea mocked them, and how the poor gentleman
roared and the bear mocked him, both roaring louder
than the sea or weather.

SHEPHERD   Name of mercy, when was this, boy?

CLOWN   Now, now; I have not winked since I saw these   100
sights. The men are not yet cold under water, nor the
bear half dined on the gentleman. He's at it now.

SHEPHERD   Would I had been by, to have helped the old
man.

CLOWN   I would you had been by the ship side, to have
helped her. There your charity would have lacked
footing.   107

SHEPHERD   Heavy matters, heavy matters! But look thee
here, boy. Now bless thyself! thou met'st with things
dying, I with things new-born. Here's a sight for thee.   110
Look thee, a bearing-cloth for a squire's child. Look   111
thee here. Take up, take up, boy; open't. So, let's see. It
was told me I should be rich by the fairies. This is some
changeling. Open't. What's within, boy?   114

CLOWN   You're a made old man. If the sins of your youth
are forgiven you, you're well to live. Gold! all gold!   116

SHEPHERD   This is fairy gold, boy, and 'twill prove so. Up
with't, keep it close. Home, home, the next way. We are   118
lucky, boy, and to be so still requires nothing but se-

---

89 *boring* piercing   **90** *yest* foam   **91** *hogshead* cask; *land service* (1) a dish of
food served on land, (2) the branch of the military serving on land rather
than on sea   **95** *flapdragoned* swallowed whole   **107** *footing* a secure place to
stand   **111** *bearing-cloth* i.e., cloth or mantle in which a child is carried to
baptism   **114** *changeling* child taken or left by fairies   **116** *well to live* well-
to-do   **118** *close* secret; *next* nearest

120   crecy. Let my sheep go. Come, good boy, the next way
home.

CLOWN   Go you the next way with your findings. I'll go
see if the bear be gone from the gentleman and how
124   much he hath eaten. They are never curst but when
they are hungry. If there be any of him left, I'll bury it.

SHEPHERD   That's a good deed. If thou mayest discern by
127   that which is left of him what he is, fetch me to the
sight of him.

CLOWN   Marry, will I; and you shall help to put him i'
130   the ground.

SHEPHERD   'Tis a lucky day, boy, and we'll do good deeds
on't.   *Exeunt.*

*

❧ **IV.1**   *Enter Time, the Chorus.*

TIME
1   I, that please some, try all, both joy and terror
2   Of good and bad, that makes and unfolds error,
Now take upon me, in the name of Time,
To use my wings. Impute it not a crime
To me or my swift passage that I slide
6   O'er sixteen years and leave the growth untried
Of that wide gap, since it is in my power
8   To o'erthrow law and in one self-born hour
9   To plant and o'erwhelm custom. Let me pass
10   The same I am, ere ancient'st order was
Or what is now received. I witness to
The times that brought them in. So shall I do
To the freshest things now reigning, and make stale
14   The glistering of this present, as my tale

---

124 *curst* mean   127 *what* who
    IV.1 1 *try* test 1–2 *joy . . . bad* joy in expectation of good fortune, and
terror at the prospect of bad 2 *unfolds* reveals 6 *growth untried* events un-
told 8 *one self-born* the very same 9 *plant and o'erwhelm* establish and
obliterate 9–11 *Let . . . received* take me for what I am, for what I have been
since before history began, before civilizations were recorded 14 *glistering*
brightness

Now seems to it. Your patience this allowing,
I turn my glass and give my scene such growing   16
As you had slept between. Leontes leaving,   17
Th' effects of his fond jealousies so grieving   18
That he shuts up himself, imagine me,
Gentle spectators, that I now may be   20
In fair Bohemia. And remember well,
I mentioned a son o' th' king's, which Florizel
I now name to you, and with speed so pace   23
To speak of Perdita, now grown in grace
Equal with wondering. What of her ensues
I list not prophesy; but let Time's news   26
Be known when 'tis brought forth. A shepherd's daughter
And what to her adheres, which follows after,   28
Is th' argument of Time. Of this allow   29
If ever you have spent time worse ere now;   30
If never, yet that Time himself doth say
He wishes earnestly you never may.   *Exit.*

                          *

∾ **IV.2** *Enter Polixenes and Camillo.*

POLIXENES   I pray thee, good Camillo, be no more im-
portunate. 'Tis a sickness denying thee anything, a
death to grant this.

CAMILLO   It is fifteen years since I saw my country.
Though I have for the most part been aired abroad, I   5
desire to lay my bones there. Besides, the penitent king,
my master, hath sent for me, to whose feeling sorrows I
might be some allay – or I o'erween to think so –   8
which is another spur to my departure.

POLIXENES   As thou lov'st me, Camillo, wipe not out the   10
rest of thy services by leaving me now. The need I have

---

16 *glass* hourglass; *scene* play; *growing* development   **17** *As* as if   **18** *fond*
foolish   **23** *pace* proceed   **26** *list not* do not wish to   **28** *adheres* relates   **29**
argument story
  IV.2 Polixenes' palace   **5** *been aired* lived   **8** *allay* comfort, relief; *o'erween*
am presumptuous

of thee thine own goodness hath made. Better not to
have had thee than thus to want thee. Thou, having
made me businesses which none without thee can suffi-
ciently manage, must either stay to execute them thyself or take away with thee the very services thou hast
done, which if I have not enough considered – as too
much I cannot – to be more thankful to thee shall be
my study, and my profit therein the heaping friendships. Of that fatal country, Sicilia, prithee speak no
more, whose very naming punishes me with the remembrance of that penitent, as thou call'st him, and
reconciled king, my brother, whose loss of his most
precious queen and children are even now to be afresh
lamented. Say to me, when saw'st thou the Prince
Florizel, my son? Kings are no less unhappy, their issue
not being gracious, than they are in losing them when
they have approved their virtues.

CAMILLO   Sir, it is three days since I saw the prince. What
his happier affairs may be, are to me unknown, but I
have missingly noted he is of late much retired from
court and is less frequent to his princely exercises than
formerly he hath appeared.

POLIXENES   I have considered so much, Camillo, and
with some care – so far that I have eyes under my service which look upon his removedness, from whom I
have this intelligence, that he is seldom from the house
of a most homely shepherd, a man, they say, that from
very nothing, and beyond the imagination of his neighbors, is grown into an unspeakable estate.

CAMILLO   I have heard, sir, of such a man, who hath a
daughter of most rare note. The report of her is ex-

---

13 *want* be without   19–20 *heaping friendships* piling up of favors and kind-
nesses   27 *gracious* pleasing, admirable, reflecting favorably on the parent
28 *approved* proved   31 *missingly* in missing him   35 *eyes* spies   35–36
under my service in my employ   36 *look . . . removedness* investigate his absence   37 *intelligence* report   38 *homely* humble   40 *unspeakable estate* un-
told wealth

tended more than can be thought to begin from such a
cottage.

POLIXENES   That's likewise part of my intelligence; but, I
fear, the angle that plucks our son thither. Thou shalt 46
accompany us to the place, where we will, not appearing what we are, have some question with the shepherd, from whose simplicity I think it not uneasy to get
the cause of my son's resort thither. Prithee be my pre- 50
sent partner in this business, and lay aside the thoughts
of Sicilia.

CAMILLO   I willingly obey your command.

POLIXENES   My best Camillo! We must disguise ourselves.   *Exeunt.*

*

∾ **IV.3** *Enter Autolycus, singing.*

AUTOLYCUS

    When daffodils begin to peer,   1
        With heigh! the doxy over the dale,   2
    Why, then comes in the sweet o' the year,
        For the red blood reigns in the winter's pale. 4

    The white sheet bleaching on the hedge,
        With heigh! the sweet birds, O how they sing!
    Doth set my pugging tooth on edge,   7
        For a quart of ale is a dish for a king.

    The lark, that tirra-lyra chants,
        With heigh! with heigh! the thrush and the jay, 10
    Are summer songs for me and my aunts,   11
        While we lie tumbling in the hay.

---

46 *angle* fishhook
    IV.3 A footpath in Bohemia **1** *peer* appear **2** *doxy* female vagrant, pros-
titute **4** *in the winter's pale* (1) instead of winter's pallor, (2) in winter's do-
main **7** *pugging* pilfering **11** *aunts* i.e., prostitutes

13   I have served Prince Florizel and in my time wore
      three-pile, but now I am out of service.

              But shall I go mourn for that, my dear?
                  The pale moon shines by night.
              And when I wander here and there,
                  I then do most go right.

              If tinkers may have leave to live,
20   And bear the sow-skin budget,
              Then my account I well may give,
22   And in the stocks avouch it.

23   My traffic is sheets; when the kite builds, look to lesser
      linen. My father named me Autolycus, who being, as I
25   am, littered under Mercury, was likewise a snapper-up
26   of unconsidered trifles. With die and drab I purchased
27   this caparison, and my revenue is the silly cheat. Gal-
      lows and knock are too powerful on the highway; beat-
      ing and hanging are terrors to me. For the life to come,
30   I sleep out the thought of it. A prize! a prize!
          Enter Clown.

13–14 *three-pile* the finest velvet   20 *bear . . . budget* carry the pigskin sack
(holding tools)   22 *stocks* (a wood frame that secured the ankles and/or
wrists, exposing and immobilizing petty criminals, who were then vulnerable
to verbal abuse and thrown objects); *avouch* testify to it   23 *traffic* trade;
sheets linen sheets (also perhaps the sheets of paper on which the ballads Autolycus sometimes sells were printed); *when the kite builds* when the kite
builds its nest nearby; *lesser* smaller pieces of (just as, when the kite builds its
nest nearby, you must keep an eye on the small pieces of linen it uses, so
when I am around, keep an eye on your sheets)   25 *littered under Mercury*
born when the planet Mercury was in the ascendant (Mercury was the god of
thieving; hence, both the earlier Autolycus, father of Odysseus, and this his
namesake are skilled in that art)   26–27 *With . . . caparison* by dice and har-
lots I got this attire   27 *revenue* source of income   27–29 *Gallows . . . me*
the prospect of hanging or being beaten scares me off being a highwayman
30 *prize* booty or one from whom it may be taken

CLOWN   Let me see; every 'leven wether tods; every tod   31
    yields pound and odd shilling; fifteen hundred shorn,
    what comes the wool to?

AUTOLYCUS   *[Aside]* If the springe hold, the cock's mine.   34

CLOWN   I cannot do't without counters. Let me see; what   35
    am I to buy for our sheepshearing feast? Three pound of
    sugar, five pound of currants, rice – what will this sister
    of mine do with rice? But my father hath made her mis-
    tress of the feast, and she lays it on. She hath made me
    four and twenty nosegays for the shearers – three-man   40
    songmen all, and very good ones; but they are most of
    them means and basses, but one puritan amongst them,   42
    and he sings psalms to hornpipes. I must have saffron to
    color the warden pies; mace; dates? – none, that's out of   44
    my note; nutmegs, seven; a race or two of ginger, but   45
    that I may beg; four pounds of prunes, and as many of
    raisins o' the sun.   47

AUTOLYCUS   O, that ever I was born!
    [Grovels on the ground.]

CLOWN   I' the name of me –

AUTOLYCUS   O, help me, help me! pluck but off these   50
    rags, and then death, death!

CLOWN   Alack, poor soul, thou hast need of more rags to
    lay on thee, rather than have these off.

AUTOLYCUS   O, sir, the loathsomeness of them offends
    me more than the stripes I have received, which are   55
    mighty ones and millions.

CLOWN   Alas, poor man! A million of beating may come
    to a great matter.

---

31 *'leven wether tods* eleven sheep yield a tod (an old weight for wool)   34
springe trap   35 *counters* disks used to keep track of sums   40–41 *three-man
songmen* men who sing in three-part harmony   42 *means* tenors   42–43
puritan . . . hornpipes except for one Puritan, who sings in the nasal, high-
pitched whine of the hornpipe, or sings psalms to the raucous music of hornpipes (a rare Shakespearean sneer at Puritans)   44 *warden* pear   44–45
out . . . note not on my list   45 *race* root   47 *o' the sun* sun-dried   55 *stripes*
welts from beatings

AUTOLYCUS   I am robbed, sir, and beaten, my money and
60   apparel ta'en from me, and these detestable things put
      upon me.
62 CLOWN   What, by a horseman, or a footman?
   AUTOLYCUS   A footman, sweet sir, a footman.
   CLOWN   Indeed, he should be a footman by the garments
      he has left with thee. If this be a horseman's coat, it
66   hath seen very hot service. Lend me thy hand, I'll help
      thee. Come, lend me thy hand.
         [Helps him up.]
   AUTOLYCUS   O, good sir, tenderly. O!
   CLOWN   Alas, poor soul!
70 AUTOLYCUS   O, good sir, softly, good sir. I fear, sir, my
      shoulder blade is out.
   CLOWN   How now? canst stand?
   AUTOLYCUS   *[Picking his pocket]* Softly, dear sir; good sir,
      softly. You ha' done me a charitable office.
   CLOWN   Dost lack any money? I have a little money for
      thee.
   AUTOLYCUS   No, good sweet sir; no, I beseech you, sir. I
      have a kinsman not past three quarters of a mile hence,
      unto whom I was going. I shall there have money, or
80   anything I want. Offer me no money, I pray you; that
      kills my heart.
   CLOWN   What manner of fellow was he that robbed you?
   AUTOLYCUS   A fellow, sir, that I have known to go about
84   with troll-my-dames. I knew him once a servant of the
      prince. I cannot tell, good sir, for which of his virtues it
      was, but he was certainly whipped out of the court.
   CLOWN   His vices, you would say. There's no virtue
      whipped out of the court. They cherish it to make it
89   stay there, and yet it will no more but abide.

---

62 *horseman* a thief on horseback; *footman* a thief on foot   **66** *hot service*
hard wear   **84** *troll-my-dames* (1) a game in which balls are rolled through
arches on a board, and players bet on the outcome, (2) prostitutes   **89** *but
abide* stay briefly or unwillingly

AUTOLYCUS　Vices, I would say, sir. I know this man well. 90
He hath been since an ape-bearer, then a process-server, 91
a bailiff. Then he compassed a motion of the Prodigal 92
Son, and married a tinker's wife within a mile where
my land and living lies, and, having flown over many
knavish professions, he settled only in rogue. Some call
him Autolycus.

CLOWN　Out upon him! Prig, for my life, prig! He 97
haunts wakes, fairs, and bearbaitings. 98

AUTOLYCUS　Very true, sir; he, sir, he. That's the rogue
that put me into this apparel. 100

CLOWN　Not a more cowardly rogue in all Bohemia. If
you had but looked big and spit at him, he'd have run.

AUTOLYCUS　I must confess to you, sir, I am no fighter. I
am false of heart that way, and that he knew, I warrant
him.

CLOWN　How do you now?

AUTOLYCUS　Sweet sir, much better than I was. I can
stand and walk. I will even take my leave of you and
pace softly towards my kinsman's.

CLOWN　Shall I bring thee on the way? 110

AUTOLYCUS　No, good-faced sir; no, sweet sir.

CLOWN　Then fare thee well. I must go buy spices for our
sheepshearing.

AUTOLYCUS　Prosper you, sweet sir.　　　　*Exit [Clown].*
Your purse is not hot enough to purchase your spice.
I'll be with you at your sheepshearing too. If I make
not this cheat bring out another and the shearers prove 117
sheep, let me be unrolled and my name put in the book 118
of virtue.

Song.

Jog on, jog on, the footpath way, 120
And merrily hent the stile-a. 121

---

91 *ape-bearer* the keeper of a trained monkey　**92** *compassed a motion* devised and put on a puppet show　**97** *Prig* thief　**98** *wakes* festivals　**117**
bring out lead to　**118** *unrolled* removed from the roll of thieves　**121** *hent*
take hold of; *stile* steps for getting over a fence

> A merry heart goes all the day,
>   Your sad tires in a mile-a.   *Exit.*

*

～ IV.4 *Enter Florizel, Perdita.*

FLORIZEL
1 These your unusual weeds to each part of you
2 Do give a life – no shepherdess, but Flora
3 Peering in April's front. This your sheepshearing
   Is as a meeting of the petty gods,
   And you the queen on't.
PERDITA   Sir, my gracious lord,
6 To chide at your extremes it not becomes me –
   O, pardon, that I name them. Your high self,
8 The gracious mark o' th' land, you have obscured
9 With a swain's wearing, and me, poor lowly maid,
10 Most goddesslike pranked up. But that our feasts
11 In every mess have folly, and the feeders
12 Digest it with a custom, I should blush
   To see you so attired, swoon, I think,
14 To show myself a glass.
FLORIZEL   I bless the time
   When my good falcon made her flight across
   Thy father's ground.
PERDITA   Now Jove afford you cause!
17 To me the difference forges dread; your greatness
   Hath not been used to fear. Even now I tremble

IV.4 The shepherd's garden **1** *weeds* clothes **1–2** *to . . . life* (Florizel may
mean that Perdita is decked with flowers head to toe) **2** *Flora* goddess of
flowers **3** *Peering* appearing; *April's front* (1) at the beginning of April, (2)
with April's face on **6** *extremes* exaggerations **8** *mark* ornament **9** *swain's
wearing* peasant's clothes **10** *pranked up* dressed up **11** *mess* group of four
served together at one table **12** *Digest . . . custom* accept it because they are
used to it **14** *glass* mirror **17** *difference . . . dread* disparity in our ranks
frightens me

To think your father, by some accident,
Should pass this way as you did. O, the Fates!   20
How would he look, to see his work, so noble,   21
Vilely bound up? What would he say? Or how   22
Should I, in these my borrowed flaunts, behold
The sternness of his presence?   24

FLORIZEL   Apprehend
Nothing but jollity. The gods themselves,
Humbling their deities to love, have taken   26
The shapes of beasts upon them. Jupiter   27
Became a bull, and bellowed; the green Neptune
A ram, and bleated; and the fire-robed god,
Golden Apollo, a poor humble swain,   30
As I seem now. Their transformations
Were never for a piece of beauty rarer,
Nor in a way so chaste, since my desires
Run not before mine honor, nor my lusts   34
Burn hotter than my faith.

PERDITA   O, but, sir,
Your resolution cannot hold when 'tis
Opposed, as it must be, by th' power of the king.
One of these two must be necessities,   38
Which then will speak, that you must change this pur-
  pose,
Or I my life.   40

FLORIZEL   Thou dearest Perdita,
With these forced thoughts, I prithee, darken not   41
The mirth o' th' feast. Or I'll be thine, my fair,   42
Or not my father's. For I cannot be
Mine own, nor anything to any, if

---

21 *work* child   22 *Vilely . . . up* cheaply bound (as a book) or dressed   24 *Apprehend* anticipate   26 *deities to* divinity in order to or because of   27–31 (Jupiter took the shape of a bull to carry off Europa, Neptune that of a man to woo Theophane; and Apollo, exiled from heaven by Jupiter, served Admetus as a shepherd and enabled him to win Alcestis)   34 *Run not before* i.e., do not win a victory over   38 *One . . . necessities* (either your resolution or the king's power must be pressing)   41 *forced* far-fetched   42 *Or* either

I be not thine. To this I am most constant,
Though destiny say no. Be merry, gentle;
Strangle such thoughts as these with anything
That you behold the while. Your guests are coming.
Lift up your countenance, as it were the day
50   Of celebration of that nuptial which
We two have sworn shall come.

PERDITA   O Lady Fortune,
Stand you auspicious!

FLORIZEL   See, your guests approach.
Address yourself to entertain them sprightly,
And let's be red with mirth.

     [Enter] Shepherd, Clown, [with] Polixenes [and]
     Camillo [disguised], Mopsa, Dorcas, Servants.

SHEPHERD
Fie, daughter! When my old wife lived, upon
56   This day she was both pantler, butler, cook,
Both dame and servant; welcomed all, served all;
Would sing her song and dance her turn; now here
At upper end o' th' table, now i' th' middle;
60   On his shoulder, and his; her face o' fire
With labor, and the thing she took to quench it
62   She would to each one sip. You are retirèd,
63   As if you were a feasted one and not
The hostess of the meeting. Pray you bid
These unknown friends to's welcome, for it is
A way to make us better friends, more known.
Come, quench your blushes and present yourself
That which you are, mistress o' th' feast. Come on,
And bid us welcome to your sheepshearing,
70   As your good flock shall prosper.

PERDITA   *[To Polixenes]*   Sir, welcome.
It is my father's will I should take on me
The hostess-ship o' th' day.

---

56 *pantler* pantry servant   **62** *to . . . sip* toast; *retirèd* withdrawn   **63** *feasted
one* i.e., guest

[To Camillo]　　　　　　You're welcome, sir.
Give me those flowers there, Dorcas. Reverend sirs,
For you there's rosemary and rue; these keep　　　　74
Seeming and savor all the winter long.　　　　75
Grace and remembrance be to you both,
And welcome to our shearing!
POLIXENES　　　　　　　　Shepherdess –
A fair one are you – well you fit our ages　　　　78
With flowers of winter.
PERDITA　　　　　　Sir, the year growing ancient,
Not yet on summer's death nor on the birth　　　　80
Of trembling winter, the fairest flowers o' th' season
Are our carnations and streaked gillyvors,　　　　82
Which some call nature's bastards. Of that kind　　　　83
Our rustic garden's barren, and I care not
To get slips of them.　　　　85
POLIXENES　　　　　Wherefore, gentle maiden,
Do you neglect them?
PERDITA　　　　　　For I have heard it said
There is an art which in their piedness shares　　　　87
With great creating nature.
POLIXENES　　　　　　　Say there be;
Yet nature is made better by no mean　　　　89
But nature makes that mean. So, over that art　　　　90
Which you say adds to nature, is an art
That nature makes. You see, sweet maid, we marry
A gentler scion to the wildest stock,　　　　93
And make conceive a bark of baser kind　　　　94
By bud of nobler race. This is an art

---

74 *rosemary . . . rue* (associated respectively with remembrance and grace)
75 *Seeming* appearance, color　78–79 *fit . . . winter* plants that survive the
winter suit older men　80–81 (it is midsummer, as she says at l. 107.)　82
gillyvors gillyflowers (clove pinks or carnations)　83 *nature's bastards* i.e., cre-
ated by crossbreeding　85 *get slips* take cuttings　87–88 *There . . . nature*
i.e., the parti-color of the flower owes as much to the skill of the gardener as
to nature　89 *mean* method　93 *scion* offshoot, heir　94 *bark* mature tree
(by metonymy)

Which does mend nature – change it rather – but
The art itself is nature.

PERDITA   So it is.

POLIXENES

Then make your garden rich in gillyvors,
And do not call them bastards.

PERDITA   I'll not put

100 The dibble in earth to set one slip of them,
101 No more than, were I painted, I would wish
This youth should say 'twere well, and only therefore
Desire to breed by me. Here's flowers for you,
104 Hot lavender, mints, savory, marjoram,
105 The marigold, that goes to bed wi' th' sun
And with him rises weeping. These are flowers
Of middle summer, and I think they are given
To men of middle age. You're very welcome.

CAMILLO

I should leave grazing, were I of your flock,
110 And only live by gazing.

PERDITA   Out, alas!
You'd be so lean that blasts of January
Would blow you through and through. Now, my fair'st
    friend,
I would I had some flowers o' th' spring that might
Become your time of day, and yours, and yours,
That wear upon your virgin branches yet
116 Your maidenheads growing. O Proserpina,
For the flowers now that, frighted, thou let'st fall
From Dis's wagon; daffodils,

---

100 *dibble* tool for making holes for seed   101 *painted* i.e., made up (with cosmetics)   104 *Hot* (herbs were thought to have temperatures)   105 *goes . . . sun* i.e., closes its petals at nightfall   116 *Proserpina* Ceres' daughter, who, spied by Dis (Pluto, god of the underworld) while she was gathering flowers, was seized and taken by him to the underworld to become his queen; ultimately, Proserpina spent six months of the year with her husband, during which time her mother grieved and the world suffered fall and winter, and six months with her mother, during which her mother rejoiced, and the earth was renewed and bountiful in spring and summer

That come before the swallow dares, and take   119
The winds of March with beauty; violets dim,   120
But sweeter than the lids of Juno's eyes   121
Or Cytherea's breath; pale primroses,   122
That die unmarried, ere they can behold   123
Bright Phoebus in his strength – a malady   124
Most incident to maids; bold oxlips and   125
The crown imperial; lilies of all kinds,   126
The flower-de-luce being one. O, these I lack   127
To make you garlands of, and my sweet friend,
To strew him o'er and o'er!   129

FLORIZEL   What, like a corse?

PERDITA
No, like a bank for love to lie and play on.   130
Not like a corse; or if, not to be buried,
But quick and in mine arms. Come, take your flowers.
Methinks I play as I have seen them do
In Whitsun pastorals. Sure this robe of mine   134
Does change my disposition.

FLORIZEL   What you do
Still betters what is done. When you speak, sweet,
I'd have you do it ever. When you sing,
I'd have you buy and sell so, so give alms,
Pray so, and for the ordering your affairs,
To sing them too. When you do dance, I wish you   140
A wave o' th' sea, that you might ever do
Nothing but that, move still, still so,

---

119 *take* charm **120** *dim* drooping **121** *Juno* wife of Jupiter and queen of heaven **122** *Cytherea* Venus **123** *die unmarried* bloom at night and die before they can be sun-kissed, or pollinated **124** *Phoebus* the sun (Phoebus Apollo, the sun god, whose oracle Leontes consults) **125** *incident to* prevalent among (Virgins were thought to be especially susceptible to chlorosis, or greensickness, a form of anemia that could best be cured by sexual activity. Legend had it that young women with this malady, who tended toward very pale complexions, could become primroses.) **126** *crown imperial* a kind of lily, popular in London gardens, which had recently been imported from Turkey **127** *flower-de-luce* fleur-de-lis, the iris **129** *corse* corpse **134** *Whitsun pastorals* plays (or morris dances) presented around Whitsun, the seventh Sunday after Easter

143 And own no other function. Each your doing,
So singular in each particular,
Crowns what you are doing in the present deeds,
146 That all your acts are queens.

PERDITA   O Doricles,
Your praises are too large. But that your youth,
148 And the true blood which peeps fairly through't,
149 Do plainly give you out an unstained shepherd,
150 With wisdom I might fear, my Doricles,
You wooed me the false way.

FLORIZEL   I think you have
152 As little skill to fear as I have purpose
To put you to't. But come; our dance, I pray.
154 Your hand, my Perdita. So turtles pair
That never mean to part.

PERDITA   I'll swear for 'em.

POLIXENES
This is the prettiest lowborn lass that ever
Ran on the greensward. Nothing she does or seems
158 But smacks of something greater than herself,
Too noble for this place.

CAMILLO   He tells her something
160 That makes her blood look on't. Good sooth, she is
The queen of curds and cream.

CLOWN   Come on, strike up!

DORCAS
Mopsa must be your mistress. Marry, garlic,
163 To mend her kissing with!

MOPSA   Now, in good time!

CLOWN
Not a word, a word! We stand upon our manners.
Come, strike up!
        [Music.] Here a dance of Shepherds and Shepherdesses.

---

143 *Each your doing* everything you do   **146** *Doricles* (the name assumed by
Florizel in his disguise)   **148** *true . . . through't* nobility that shines beauti-
fully through it   **149** *unstained* pure, virginal   **152** *skill* reason   **154** *turtles*
turtledoves   **158** *greater* of gentler blood   **160** *blood look on't* blush   **163**
mend . . . with escape her unpleasant breath

POLIXENES

  Pray, good shepherd, what fair swain is this

  Which dances with your daughter?

SHEPHERD

  They call him Doricles, and boasts himself

  To have a worthy feeding. But I have it   169

  Upon his own report and I believe it;   *170*

  He looks like sooth. He says he loves my daughter.   171

  I think so too, for never gazed the moon

  Upon the water as he'll stand and read

  As 'twere my daughter's eyes; and, to be plain,

  I think there is not half a kiss to choose

  Who loves another best.   176

POLIXENES   She dances featly.

SHEPHERD

  So she does anything, though I report it

  That should be silent. If young Doricles

  Do light upon her, she shall bring him that   179

  Which he not dreams of.   *180*

    Enter Servant.

SERVANT O master, if you did but hear the pedlar at the door, you would never dance again after a tabor and pipe – no, the bagpipe could not move you. He sings several tunes faster than you'll tell money. He utters 184 them as he had eaten ballads and all men's ears grew to 185 his tunes.

CLOWN He could never come better. He shall come in. I 187 love a ballad but even too well if it be doleful matter merrily set down, or a very pleasant thing indeed and sung lamentably.   *190*

SERVANT He hath songs for man or woman, of all sizes. No milliner can so fit his customers with gloves. He has the prettiest love songs for maids, so without bawdry,

---

169 *feeding* land on which sheep feed **171** *like sooth* honest **176** *another* the other; *featly* nimbly **179** *light upon* end up with, make a match with **184** *tell* count **185** *as . . . ballads* as if he had lived on ballads – i.e., the cheaply printed sheets of popular song lyrics hawked across the countryside by peddlers like Autolycus; *grew to* listened to **187** *better* at a better time

194   which is strange, with such delicate burdens of dildos
195   and fadings, "Jump her and thump her." And where
196   some stretch-mouthed rascal would, as it were, mean
197   mischief and break a foul gap into the matter, he makes
       the maid to answer, "Whoop, do me no harm, good
       man"; puts him off, slights him, with "Whoop, do me
200   no harm, good man."
201   POLIXENES   This is a brave fellow.
202   CLOWN   Believe me, thou talkest of an admirable con-
203   ceited fellow. Has he any unbraided wares?
       SERVANT   He hath ribbons of all the colors i' th' rainbow,
205   points more than all the lawyers in Bohemia can
          learnedly handle, though they come to him by the
207   gross – inkles, caddises, cambrics, lawns. Why, he sings
          'em over as they were gods or goddesses. You would
          think a smock were a she-angel, he so chants to the
210   sleevehand and the work about the square on't.
       CLOWN   Prithee bring him in, and let him approach
          singing.
       PERDITA   Forewarn him that he use no scurrilous words
          in's tunes.   [Exit Servant.]
215   CLOWN   You have of these peddlers that have more in
          them than you'd think, sister.
217   PERDITA   Ay, good brother, or go about to think.
          Enter Autolycus, singing.
       AUTOLYCUS
                   Lawn as white as driven snow,
219   Cyprus black as e'er was crow,

---

194 *burdens* refrains; *dildos* (1) a nonsense word used as a refrain in ballads,
(2) a fake penis   195 *fadings* (1) refrains, (2) orgasms   193–95 (although the
servant insists that the songs are *without bawdry*, many of his terms have sexual connotations)   196 *stretch-mouthed* foul-mouthed   197 *break . . . matter* rudely interrupt   201 *brave* impudent, bawdy   202–3 *conceited* witty
203 *unbraided* unfaded, new   205 *points* (1) laces to fasten doublet and hose
together, (2) points in an argument   207 *inkles* linen tape; *caddises* worsted
ribbons; *cambrics* heavy linens; *lawns* sheer linens   207–8 *sings . . . goddesses*
recites the names as if it were a litany of worship   210 *sleevehand* cuff;
work needlework; *square* the front yoke of a dress   215 *You have* there are
some   217 *go about to* want to   219 *Cyprus* cloth from Cyprus

> Gloves as sweet as damask roses,   *220*
> Masks for faces and for noses,
> Bugle bracelet, necklace amber,   *222*
> Perfume for a lady's chamber,
> Golden quoifs and stomachers   *224*
> For my lads to give their dears,
> Pins and poking sticks of steel,   *226*
> What maids lack from head to heel.
> Come buy of me, come; come buy, come buy.
> Buy, lads, or else your lasses cry.
> Come buy.   *230*

CLOWN   If I were not in love with Mopsa, thou shouldst take no money of me; but being enthralled as I am, it will also be the bondage of certain ribbons and gloves.   *233*

MOPSA   I was promised them against the feast, but they *234* come not too late now.

DORCAS   He hath promised you more than that, or there be liars.

MOPSA   He hath paid you all he promised you. May be he has paid you more, which will shame you to give him *239* again.   *240*

CLOWN   Is there no manners left among maids? Will they wear their plackets where they should bear their *242* faces? Is there not milking time, when you are going to bed, or kiln hole, to whistle of these secrets, but you *244* must be tittle-tattling before all our guests? 'Tis well they are whispering. Clamor your tongues, and not a *246* word more.

---

222 *Bugle* bead   224 *quoifs* coifs, headdresses; *stomachers* stiff embroidered bodices   226 *poking sticks* metal rods used to iron pleats, or, figuratively, penises   233 *bondage . . . gloves* ribbons and gloves will also have to be tied up (in parcels)   234 *against* in time for   239–40 *to give him again* into giving back to him (implying that Dorcas has had sex with the clown, Mopsa also suggests that the result might be an illegitimate child)   242–43 *wear . . . faces* brazenly display their underwear or genitals (i.e., their private business)   244 *kiln hole* fireplace or oven, or, figuratively, the vagina (?)   246 *Clamor* stop (?)

248 MOPSA   I have done. Come, you promised me a tawdry
249   lace and a pair of sweet gloves.

250 CLOWN   Have I not told thee how I was cozened by the
    way and lost all my money?

    AUTOLYCUS   And indeed, sir, there are cozeners abroad;
    therefore it behoves men to be wary.

    CLOWN   Fear not thou, man; thou shalt lose nothing
    here.

    AUTOLYCUS   I hope so, sir, for I have about me many
257   parcels of charge.

    CLOWN   What hast here? Ballads?

259 MOPSA   Pray now, buy some. I love a ballad in print, a
260   life, for then we are sure they are true.

    AUTOLYCUS   Here's one to a very doleful tune, how a
    usurer's wife was brought to bed of twenty moneybags
263   at a burden, and how she longed to eat adders' heads
264   and toads carbonadoed.

    MOPSA   Is it true, think you?

    AUTOLYCUS   Very true, and but a month old.

    DORCAS   Bless me from marrying a usurer!

    AUTOLYCUS   Here's the midwife's name to't, one Mistress
269   Tale-porter, and five or six honest wives that were pre-
270   sent. Why should I carry lies abroad?

    MOPSA   Pray you now, buy it.

    CLOWN   Come on, lay it by. And let's first see moe bal-
    lads; we'll buy the other things anon.

    AUTOLYCUS   Here's another ballad of a fish that appeared
275   upon the coast on Wednesday the fourscore of April,
    forty thousand fathom above water, and sung this bal-
    lad against the hard hearts of maids. It was thought she
    was a woman and was turned into a cold fish for she

248–49 *tawdry lace* colored neckerchief   249 *sweet* scented   250 *cozened*
cheated   257 *charge* value   259–60 *a life* on my life   263 *at a burden* at
once in a litter or by bearing the sexual burden of a high-paying customer
264 *carbonadoed* grilled   269 *Tale-porter* (the name suggests both a tale re-
porter, or gossip, and a tail carrier, or bawd, who trades in female genitals, or
"tails")   275–76 *fourscore . . . water* (parody of the kind of "wonders" de-
picted in broadside ballads)

would not exchange flesh with one that loved her. The   279
ballad is very pitiful and as true.   280

DORCAS   Is it true too, think you?

AUTOLYCUS   Five justices' hands at it, and witnesses more
than my pack will hold.

CLOWN   Lay it by too. Another.

AUTOLYCUS   This is a merry ballad, but a very pretty one.

MOPSA   Let's have some merry ones.

AUTOLYCUS   Why, this is a passing merry one and goes to
the tune of "Two maids wooing a man." There's scarce
a maid westward but she sings it. 'Tis in request, I can   289
tell you.   290

MOPSA   We can both sing it; if thou'lt bear a part, thou   291
shalt hear. 'Tis in three parts.

DORCAS   We had the tune on't a month ago.

AUTOLYCUS   I can bear my part; you must know 'tis my
occupation. Have at it with you.

Song.

AUTOLYCUS	Get you hence, for I must go
	Where it fits not you to know.
DORCAS	Whither?
MOPSA	O, whither?
DORCAS	Whither?
MOPSA	It becomes thy oath full well,
	Thou to me thy secrets tell.
DORCAS	Me too; let me go thither.
MOPSA	Or thou goest to th' grange or mill.
DORCAS	If to either, thou dost ill.
AUTOLYCUS	Neither.
DORCAS	What, neither?
AUTOLYCUS	Neither.
DORCAS	Thou hast sworn my love to be.

(line numbers: 300 at "Thou to me thy secrets tell."; 302 at "Or thou goest to th' grange or mill.")

---

279 *exchange flesh* have intercourse   **289** *westward* (in England the "un-
spoiled" country)   **291** *bear a part* join in sex, as well as song   **302** *grange*
farm

MOPSA   Thou hast sworn it more to me.
                       Then whither goest? say, whither?
CLOWN   We'll have this song out anon by ourselves. My
father and the gentlemen are in sad talk, and we'll not
trouble them. Come, bring away thy pack after me.
Wenches, I'll buy for you both. Pedlar, let's have the
first choice. Follow me, girls.
                       [Exit with Dorcas and Mopsa.]
AUTOLYCUS   And you shall pay well for 'em.
         [Follows singing.]

                       Song.

               Will you buy any tape,
               Or lace for your cape,
               My dainty duck, my dear-a?
                  Any silk, any thread,
                  Any toys for your head
               Of the new'st and fin'st, fin'st wear-a?
                     Come to the peddler.
                     Money 's a meddler
                  That doth utter all men's ware-a.   *Exit.*
         [Enter Servant.]

SERVANT   Master, there is three carters, three shepherds,
three neatherds, three swineherds, that have made
themselves all men of hair. They call themselves
Saltiers, and they have a dance which the wenches say is
a gallimaufry of gambols, because they are not in't; but
they themselves are o' th' mind, if it be not too rough
for some that know little but bowling, it will please
plentifully.
SHEPHERD   Away! we'll none on't. Here has been too
much homely foolery already. I know, sir, we weary
you.

---

309 *sad* serious   318 *toys* trinkets   322 *utter* sell   323 *carters* those who
drive carts   324 *neatherds* cowherds   325 *of hair* i.e., wearing skins of ani-
mals   326 *Saltiers* i.e., satyrs   327 *gallimaufry* hodgepodge   332 *homely*
lacking refinement

POLIXENES   You weary those that refresh us. Pray, let's
see these four threes of herdsmen.

SERVANT   One three of them, by their own report, sir, 336
hath danced before the king; and not the worst of the
three but jumps twelve foot and a half by th' squire. 338

SHEPHERD   Leave your prating. Since these good men
are pleased, let them come in; but quickly now. 340

SERVANT   Why, they stay at door, sir. *[Exit.]*
Here a dance of twelve Satyrs.

POLIXENES
O, father, you'll know more of that hereafter.
[To Camillo]
Is it not too far gone? 'Tis time to part them.
He's simple and tells much. – How now, fair shepherd,
Your heart is full of something that does take
Your mind from feasting. Sooth, when I was young
And handed love as you do, I was wont 347
To load my she with knacks. I would have ransacked 348
The pedlar's silken treasury and have poured it
To her acceptance. You have let him go 350
And nothing marted with him. If your lass 351
Interpretation should abuse and call this 352
Your lack of love or bounty, you were straited 353
For a reply, at least if you make a care 354
Of happy holding her.

FLORIZEL   Old sir, I know
She prizes not such trifles as these are.
The gifts she looks from me are packed and locked
Up in my heart, which I have given already,
But not delivered. O, hear me breathe my life 359
Before this ancient sir, who, it should seem, 360
Hath sometime loved. I take thy hand, this hand
As soft as dove's down and as white as it,

---

336 *One three* one group of three   338 *squire* square (cf. T square)   347
handed pledged by the hand   348 *she . . . knacks* girlfriend with knick-
knacks, little gifts   350 *To . . . acceptance* for her approval   351 *marted*
traded   352 *Interpretation . . . abuse* misinterpret   353 *straited* hard pressed
354 *care* serious wish   359 *breathe . . . life* vow

363 Or Ethiopian's tooth, or the fanned snow that's bolted
By th' northern blasts twice o'er.

POLIXENES   What follows this?
How prettily the young swain seems to wash
The hand was fair before! I have put you out.
But to your protestation; let me hear
What you profess.

FLORIZEL   Do, and be witness to't.

POLIXENES
And this my neighbor too?

FLORIZEL   And he, and more
370 Than he, and men, the earth, the heavens, and all –
That, were I crowned the most imperial monarch,
Thereof most worthy, were I the fairest youth
That ever made eye swerve, had force and knowledge
More than was ever man's, I would not prize them
Without her love; for her, employ them all;
376 Commend them and condemn them to her service
Or to their own perdition.

POLIXENES   Fairly offered.

CAMILLO
This shows a sound affection.

SHEPHERD   But, my daughter,
Say you the like to him?

PERDITA   I cannot speak
380 So well, nothing so well; no, nor mean better.
By th' pattern of mine own thoughts I cut out
The purity of his.

SHEPHERD   Take hands, a bargain!
And, friends unknown, you shall bear witness to't.
I give my daughter to him and will make
Her portion equal his.

FLORIZEL   O, that must be
I' th' virtue of your daughter. One being dead,
I shall have more than you can dream of yet,

---

363 *fanned* blown; *bolted* sifted   **376** *condemn* i.e., to *perdition*

Enough then for your wonder. But, come on,
Contract us 'fore these witnesses.

SHEPHERD   Come, your hand;
And, daughter, yours.   390

POLIXENES   Soft, swain, awhile, beseech you.
Have you a father?

FLORIZEL   I have, but what of him?

POLIXENES
Knows he of this?

FLORIZEL   - He neither does nor shall.

POLIXENES
Methinks a father
Is at the nuptial of his son a guest
That best becomes the table. Pray you once more,
Is not your father grown incapable
Of reasonable affairs? Is he not stupid   397
With age and altering rheums? Can he speak? hear? 398
Know man from man? dispute his own estate?   399
Lies he not bed-rid? and again does nothing   400
But what he did being childish?

FLORIZEL   No, good sir,
He has his health and ampler strength indeed
Than most have of his age.

POLIXENES   By my white beard,
You offer him, if this be so, a wrong
Something unfilial. Reason my son   405
Should choose himself a wife, but as good reason
The father, all whose joy is nothing else
But fair posterity, should hold some counsel
In such a business.

FLORIZEL   I yield all this;
But for some other reasons, my grave sir,   410
Which 'tis not fit you know, I not acquaint   411
My father of this business.

---

390 *Soft* not so fast 397 *reasonable affairs* affairs requiring reason 398 *altering rheums* disabling diseases 399 *Dispute* discuss 405 *Something* somewhat; *Reason* it is reasonable 411 *not* i.e., cannot

POLIXENES   Let him know't.

FLORIZEL

   He shall not.

POLIXENES   Prithee, let him.

FLORIZEL   No, he must not.

SHEPHERD

   Let him, my son. He shall not need to grieve

   At knowing of thy choice.

FLORIZEL   Come, come, he must not.

   Mark our contract.

POLIXENES   Mark your divorce, young sir,

   [Removes his disguise.]

   Whom son I dare not call. Thou art too base

   To be acknowledged. Thou a scepter's heir,

   That thus affects a sheephook! – Thou old traitor,

420   I am sorry that by hanging thee I can

421   But shorten thy life one week. – And thou, fresh piece

422   Of excellent witchcraft, who of force must know

423   The royal fool thou cop'st with –

SHEPHERD   O, my heart!

POLIXENES

   I'll have thy beauty scratched with briers, and made

425   More homely than thy state. – For thee, fond boy,

   If I may ever know thou dost but sigh

427   That thou no more shalt see this knack – as never

   I mean thou shalt – we'll bar thee from succession,

   Not hold thee of our blood – no, not our kin –

430   Farre than Deucalion off. Mark thou my words.

431   Follow us to the court. – Thou churl, for this time,

---

421 *fresh piece* young woman   422 *excellent witchcraft* bewitching seduction; *of force* perforce   423 *cop'st with* deals with, has sex with   425 *fond* foolish 427 *knack* trifle   430 *Farre* farther; *Deucalion* (According to Greek mythology this king of Thessaly and his wife were the only human beings to escape a flood sent by Zeus, and were therefore particularly distant relatives. Deucalion is a figure similar to Noah in the Old Testament.)   431 *churl* low-status person, a peasant (an insult meant to emphasize the disparity between the king and the shepherd)

Though full of our displeasure, yet we free thee
From the dead blow of it. – And you, enchantment,   433
Worthy enough a herdsman – yea, him too,
That makes himself, but for our honor therein,
Unworthy thee – if ever henceforth thou
These rural latches to his entrance open,   437
Or hoop his body more with thy embraces,   438
I will devise a death as cruel for thee
As thou art tender to't.   *Exit.*   440

PERDITA   Even here undone!
I was not much afeard; for once or twice
I was about to speak and tell him plainly
The selfsame sun that shines upon his court
Hides not his visage from our cottage but
Looks on alike. Will't please you, sir, be gone?   445
I told you what would come of this. Beseech you,
Of your own state take care. This dream of mine –
Being now awake, I'll queen it no inch farther,
But milk my ewes and weep.

CAMILLO   Why, how now, father?
Speak ere thou diest.   450

SHEPHERD   I cannot speak, nor think,
Nor dare to know that which I know. O sir,
You have undone a man of fourscore three,   452
That thought to fill his grave in quiet, yea,
To die upon the bed my father died,   454
To lie close by his honest bones; but now
Some hangman must put on my shroud and lay me
Where no priest shovels in dust. O cursèd wretch,
That knew'st this was the prince, and wouldst adventure

---

433 *dead* death-dealing; *enchantment* charmer – i.e., both a sorcerer and a se-
ducer (here, as in IV.4.422, Polixenes simultaneously accuses Perdita of bewitching Florizel and acknowledges her attractiveness)   **437** *rural latches . . .
open* (referring to both welcoming Florizel into the cottage and allowing him
entrance sexually)   **438** *hoop* enclose   **440** *tender* vulnerable   **445** *Looks on
alike* shines on us both   **452** *fourscore three* eighty-three   **454** *died* i.e., died
upon

459   To mingle faith with him. Undone! undone!
460   If I might die within this hour, I have lived
       To die when I desire.   *Exit.*

FLORIZEL   Why look you so upon me?
       I am but sorry, not afeard; delayed,
       But nothing altered. What I was, I am,
464   More straining on for plucking back, not following
       My leash unwillingly.

CAMILLO   Gracious my lord,
       You know your father's temper. At this time
       He will allow no speech, which I do guess
       You do not purpose to him; and as hardly
       Will he endure your sight as yet, I fear.
470   Then, till the fury of his highness settle,
       Come not before him.

FLORIZEL   I not purpose it.
       I think – Camillo?

CAMILLO   Even he, my lord.

PERDITA
       How often have I told you 'twould be thus?
474   How often said my dignity would last
       But till 'twere known!

FLORIZEL   It cannot fail but by
       The violation of my faith; and then
       Let nature crush the sides o' th' earth together
       And mar the seeds within. Lift up thy looks.
       From my succession wipe me, father. I
480   Am heir to my affection.

CAMILLO   Be advised.

FLORIZEL
481   I am, and by my fancy. If my reason
       Will thereto be obedient, I have reason;

---

459 *mingle faith* exchange vows   464 *straining . . . back* more eager to proceed for having been opposed 464–65 *following . . . unwillingly* i.e., dragged
along   474 *dignity* i.e., honor of being the prince's betrothed   481 *fancy*
love

If not, my senses, better pleased with madness,
Do bid it welcome.
CAMILLO   This is desperate, sir.
FLORIZEL
So call it, but it does fulfill my vow.
I needs must think it honesty. Camillo,
Not for Bohemia nor the pomp that may
Be thereat gleaned, for all the sun sees or
The close earth wombs or the profound seas hide   489
In unknown fathoms, will I break my oath   490
To this my fair beloved. Therefore, I pray you,
As you have ever been my father's honored friend,
When he shall miss me – as, in faith, I mean not
To see him any more – cast your good counsels
Upon his passion. Let myself and fortune
Tug for the time to come. This you may know   496
And so deliver: I am put to sea
With her who here I cannot hold on shore.
And most opportune to her need I have
A vessel rides fast by, but not prepared   500
For this design. What course I mean to hold
Shall nothing benefit your knowledge, nor   502
Concern me the reporting.
CAMILLO   O my lord,
I would your spirit were easier for advice   504
Or stronger for your need.
FLORIZEL   Hark, Perdita.
   [Draws her aside.]
I'll hear you by and by.   506
CAMILLO   He's irremovable,
Resolved for flight. Now were I happy if
His going I could frame to serve my turn,

---

489 *wombs* encloses 496 *Tug* contend 502–3 *Shall . . . reporting* it does
not behoove you to know or me to say 504–5 *easier . . . need* more recep-
tive to advice or more up to this challenge 506 *irremovable* immovable, im-
placable

Save him from danger, do him love and honor,
510 Purchase the sight again of dear Sicilia
And that unhappy king, my master, whom
I so much thirst to see.

FLORIZEL   Now, good Camillo.
513 I am so fraught with curious business that
I leave out ceremony.

CAMILLO   Sir, I think
You have heard of my poor services i' th' love
That I have borne your father?

FLORIZEL   Very nobly
Have you deserved. It is my father's music
518 To speak your deeds, not little of his care
To have them recompensed as thought on.

CAMILLO   Well, my lord,
520 If you may please to think I love the king
And, through him, what's nearest to him, which is
522 Your gracious self, embrace but my direction.
If your more ponderous and settled project
May suffer alteration, on mine honor,
I'll point you where you shall have such receiving
As shall become your highness, where you may
527 Enjoy your mistress, from the whom, I see,
There's no disjunction to be made but by –
As heavens forfend! – your ruin; marry her,
530 And, with my best endeavors in your absence,
531 Your discontenting father strive to qualify
And bring him up to liking.

FLORIZEL   How, Camillo,
May this, almost a miracle, be done?
That I may call thee something more than man,
And after that trust to thee.

---

513 *curious* requiring care   518–19 *not . . . on* no small concern to have your deeds as well rewarded as they are highly regarded   522 *embrace . . . direction* accept my advice   527–28 *from . . . made* from whom you cannot be parted   531 *qualify* assuage

CAMILLO   Have you thought on
  A place whereto you'll go?
FLORIZEL   Not any yet.
  But as th' unthought-on accident is guilty   537
  To what we wildly do, so we profess
  Ourselves to be the slaves of chance, and flies
  Of every wind that blows.   540
CAMILLO   Then list to me.
  This follows: if you will not change your purpose
  But undergo this flight, make for Sicilia,
  And there present yourself and your fair princess,
  For so I see she must be, 'fore Leontes.
  She shall be habited as it becomes
  The partner of your bed. Methinks I see
  Leontes opening his free arms and weeping   547
  His welcomes forth; asks thee the son forgiveness,
  As 'twere i' th' father's person; kisses the hands
  Of your fresh princess; o'er and o'er divides him   550
  'Twixt his unkindness and his kindness; th' one
  He chides to hell and bids the other grow
  Faster than thought or time.
FLORIZEL   Worthy Camillo,
  What color for my visitation shall I   554
  Hold up before him?
CAMILLO   Sent by the king your father
  To greet him and to give him comforts. Sir,
  The manner of your bearing towards him, with
  What you, as from your father, shall deliver,
  Things known betwixt us three, I'll write you down,
  The which shall point you forth at every sitting   560
  What you must say, that he shall not perceive

537–38 *unthought-on . . . do* i.e., his unforeseen discovery by his father is to blame for what he rashly does 547 *free* hospitable 550–51 *divides . . . kindness* alternates between lamenting his past unkindness to your father and expressing the kindness he feels toward you now 554 *color* pretext 560 *point . . . sitting* guide you at every interview

562 But that you have your father's bosom there
And speak his very heart.

FLORIZEL   I am bound to you.

564 There is some sap in this.

CAMILLO   A course more promising
Than a wild dedication of yourselves
To unpathed waters, undreamed shores, most certain
To miseries enough; no hope to help you,
But as you shake off one to take another;
Nothing so certain as your anchors, who

570 Do their best office if they can but stay you
Where you'll be loath to be. Besides, you know
Prosperity's the very bond of love,
Whose fresh complexion and whose heart together
Affliction alters.

PERDITA   One of these is true.
I think affliction may subdue the cheek

576 But not take in the mind.

CAMILLO   Yea, say you so?

577 There shall not at your father's house these seven years
Be born another such.

FLORIZEL   My good Camillo,

579 She's as forward of her breeding as
580 She is i' th' rear 'our birth.

CAMILLO   I cannot say 'tis pity

581 She lacks instructions, for she seems a mistress
To most that teach.

PERDITA   Your pardon, sir. For this
I'll blush you thanks.

FLORIZEL   My prettiest Perdita!
But O, the thorns we stand upon! Camillo,
Preserver of my father, now of me,

586 The medicine of our house, how shall we do?

---

562 *bosom* confidence   564 *sap* life, potential   570 *stay* hold   576 *take in* subdue   577 *these seven years* i.e., for a long time to come (*seven* not to be taken literally)   579 *forward of* beyond   580 *'our* of our   581 *instructions* schooling   586 *medicine* physician

We are not furnished like Bohemia's son,
Nor shall appear in Sicilia.   588
CAMILLO　　　　　　　　　　My lord,
  Fear none of this. I think you know my fortunes
  Do all lie there. It shall be so my care   590
  To have you royally appointed as if
  The scene you play were mine. For instance, sir,
  That you may know you shall not want, one word.
    [They talk aside.] Enter Autolycus.
AUTOLYCUS　Ha, ha, what a fool Honesty is! and Trust,
  his sworn brother, a very simple gentleman! I have sold
  all my trumpery. Not a counterfeit stone, not a ribbon,
  glass, pomander, brooch, table book, ballad, knife,   597
  tape, glove, shoe tie, bracelet, horn ring, to keep my   598
  pack from fasting. They throng who should buy first, as
  if my trinkets had been hallowed and brought a bene-   600
  diction to the buyer; by which means I saw whose
  purse was best in picture, and what I saw, to my good   602
  use I remembered. My clown, who wants but something to be a reasonable man, grew so in love with the
  wenches' song that he would not stir his pettitoes till he 605
  had both tune and words, which so drew the rest of the
  herd to me that all their other senses stuck in ears. You   607
  might have pinched a placket, it was senseless; 'twas   608
  nothing to geld a codpiece of a purse; I would have   609
  filed keys off that hung in chains. No hearing, no feel-   610
  ing, but my sir's song and admiring the nothing of it.   611
  So that in this time of lethargy I picked and cut most of
  their festival purses; and had not the old man come in
  with a whoo-bub against his daughter and the king's

---

588 *appear* i.e., as the king's son　**597** *pomander* a scented ball worn on the
body to ward off infections; *table book* notebook　**598–99** *keep . . . fasting*
i.e., he has sold everything so his pack will go hungry　**602** *was best in picture* looked best　**605** *pettitoes* toes (usually of a pig)　**607** *stuck in ears* were
devoted to listening　**608** *placket* (1) woman's undergarment, (2) genitals;
senseless without feeling　**609** *nothing . . . purse* it was easy to cut off a purse
hanging from the pouch men wore covering their genitals (i.e., to castrate
men of their purses)　**611** *my sir's* i.e., the clown's

615 son and scared my choughs from the chaff, I had not
left a purse alive in the whole army.
    [Camillo, Florizel, and Perdita come forward.]
CAMILLO
Nay, but my letters, by this means being there
So soon as you arrive, shall clear that doubt.
FLORIZEL
And those that you'll procure from King Leontes –
CAMILLO
620 Shall satisfy your father.
PERDITA   Happy be you!
All that you speak shows fair.
CAMILLO   *[Seeing Autolycus]*   Who have we here?
622 We'll make an instrument of this, omit
Nothing may give us aid.
AUTOLYCUS   If they have overheard me now, why,
hanging.
CAMILLO
How now, good fellow? Why shakest thou so?
Fear not, man; here's no harm intended to thee.
AUTOLYCUS   I am a poor fellow, sir.
CAMILLO   Why, be so still; here's nobody will steal that
630 from thee. Yet for the outside of thy poverty we must
631 make an exchange. Therefore discase thee instantly –
thou must think there's a necessity in't – and change
633 garments with this gentleman. Though the penny-
worth on his side be the worst, yet hold thee, there's
635 some boot.
AUTOLYCUS   I am a poor fellow, sir. *[Aside]* I know ye
well enough.
638 CAMILLO   Nay, prithee, dispatch. The gentleman is half
639 flayed already.

---

615 *choughs* birds of the crow family   **622** *instrument* means to an end   **630**
the outside . . . poverty your rags   **631** *discase* undress   **633–34** *Though . . .*
worst though he gets the worse in the exchange   **635** *boot* i.e., something additional (usually to equalize an exchange)   **638** *dispatch* make haste   **639**
flayed skinned

AUTOLYCUS   Are you in earnest, sir? *[Aside]* I smell the 640
trick on't.

FLORIZEL   Dispatch, I prithee.

AUTOLYCUS   Indeed, I have had earnest, but I cannot 643
with conscience take it.

CAMILLO   Unbuckle, unbuckle.
[Florizel and Autolycus exchange garments.]
Fortunate mistress – let my prophecy
Come home to ye! – you must retire yourself 647
Into some covert. Take your sweetheart's hat 648
And pluck it o'er your brows, muffle your face,
Dismantle you, and, as you can, disliken 650
The truth of your own seeming, that you may –
For I do fear eyes over – to shipboard 652
Get undescried. 653

PERDITA   I see the play so lies
That I must bear a part.

CAMILLO   No remedy.
Have you done there?

FLORIZEL   Should I now meet my father,
He would not call me son.

CAMILLO   Nay, you shall have no hat.
[Gives it to Perdita.]
Come, lady, come. Farewell, my friend.

AUTOLYCUS   Adieu, sir.

FLORIZEL
O Perdita, what have we twain forgot?
Pray you, a word.

CAMILLO   *[Aside]*
What I do next, shall be to tell the king 660
Of this escape and whither they are bound;
Wherein my hope is I shall so prevail
To force him after; in whose company

---

643 *earnest* partial prepayment   647 *Come . . . ye* be fulfilled   648 *covert*
hiding place   650–51 *as . . . seeming* as far as you can, alter your true appearance   652 *eyes over* spying   653 *undescried* unnoticed, unrecognized

I shall review Sicilia, for whose sight
665   I have a woman's longing.

FLORIZEL   Fortune speed us!
Thus we set on, Camillo, to the seaside.

CAMILLO
The swifter speed the better.

             Exeunt [Florizel, Perdita, and Camillo].

AUTOLYCUS   I understand the business, I hear it. To have
an open ear, a quick eye, and a nimble hand is neces-
670   sary for a cutpurse. A good nose is requisite also, to
smell out work for the other senses. I see this is the time
that the unjust man doth thrive. What an exchange had
this been without boot! What a boot is here with this
exchange! Sure the gods do this year connive at us, and
675   we may do anything extempore. The prince himself is
about a piece of iniquity, stealing away from his father
677   with his clog at his heels. If I thought it were a piece of
honesty to acquaint the king withal, I would not do't. I
hold it the more knavery to conceal it, and therein am I
680   constant to my profession.

    Enter Clown and Shepherd.

Aside, aside! Here is more matter for a hot brain. Every
lane's end, every shop, church, session, hanging, yields
a careful man work.

CLOWN   See, see! What a man you are now! There is no
685   other way but to tell the king she's a changeling and
none of your flesh and blood.

SHEPHERD   Nay, but hear me.

CLOWN   Nay, but hear me.

689   SHEPHERD   Go to, then.

690   CLOWN   She being none of your flesh and blood, your
flesh and blood has not offended the king, and so your

---

665 *longing* (as for particular foods during pregnancy)   **675** *extempore* spon-
taneously   **677** *clog* (anything that impedes movement – i.e., a "ball and
chain")   **685** *changeling* a child left (by fairies) with other than its true parents   **689** *Go to* go on

flesh and blood is not to be punished by him. Show
those things you found about her, those secret things,
all but what she has with her. This being done, let the
law go whistle, I warrant you.

SHEPHERD   I will tell the king all, every word – yea, and
his son's pranks too, who, I may say, is no honest man,
neither to his father nor to me, to go about to make me
the king's brother-in-law.

CLOWN   Indeed, brother-in-law was the farthest off you   *700*
could have been to him, and then your blood had been
the dearer by I know how much an ounce.   *702*

AUTOLYCUS   *[Aside]* Very wisely, puppies.

SHEPHERD   Well, let us to the king. There is that in this
fardel will make him scratch his beard.   *705*

AUTOLYCUS   *[Aside]* I know not what impediment this
complaint may be to the flight of my master.

CLOWN   Pray heartily he be at' palace.   *708*

AUTOLYCUS   *[Aside]* Though I am not naturally honest, I
am so sometimes by chance. Let me pocket up my ped-   *710*
dler's excrement. *[Takes off his false beard.]* How now, *711*
rustics, whither are you bound?

SHEPHERD   To the palace, an it like your worship.   *713*

AUTOLYCUS   Your affairs there, what, with whom, the
condition of that fardel, the place of your dwelling,
your names, your ages, of what having, breeding, and   *716*
anything that is fitting to be known, discover.   *717*

CLOWN   We are but plain fellows, sir.

AUTOLYCUS   A lie! You are rough and hairy. Let me have
no lying. It becomes none but tradesmen, and they   *720*
often give us soldiers the lie; but we pay them for it   *721*
with stamped coin, not stabbing steel; therefore they
do not give us the lie.

---

702 *the dearer* of greater worth   705 *fardel* bundle   708 *at'* at the   711 *ex-*
crement hair (hair and nails were called excrements, since they grew out of
the body)   713 *an it like* if it please   716 *having* property   717 *discover* reveal   721 *give . . . lie* insult or cheat (since we pay them for their abuse, they
do not give us anything)

724 CLOWN   Your worship had like to have given us one, if
725   you had not taken yourself with the manner.

SHEPHERD   Are you a courtier, an't like you, sir?

AUTOLYCUS   Whether it like me or no, I am a courtier.
728   Seest thou not the air of the court in these enfoldings?
   Hath not my gait in it the measure of the court? Re-
730   ceives not thy nose court odor from me? Reflect I not
   on thy baseness, court contempt? Thinkest thou, for
732   that I insinuate, or toaze from thee thy business, I
733   am therefore no courtier? I am courtier cap-à-pie, and
   one that will either push on or pluck back thy business
   there. Whereupon I command thee to open thy affair.

SHEPHERD   My business, sir, is to the king.

AUTOLYCUS   What advocate hast thou to him?

SHEPHERD   I know not, an't like you.

739 CLOWN   Advocate's the court word for a pheasant. Say
740   you have none.

SHEPHERD   None, sir. I have no pheasant, cock nor hen.

AUTOLYCUS
   How blessed are we that are not simple men!
   Yet nature might have made me as these are;
   Therefore I will not disdain.

CLOWN   This cannot be but a great courtier.

SHEPHERD   His garments are rich, but he wears them not
   handsomely.

CLOWN   He seems to be the more noble in being
749   fantastical. A great man, I'll warrant. I know by the
750   picking on's teeth.

AUTOLYCUS   The fardel there? What's i' the fardel?
   Wherefore that box?

SHEPHERD   Sir, there lies such secrets in this fardel and
   box, which none must know but the king, and which

---

724 *one* a lie   725 *taken . . . manner* caught yourself in the act   728 *enfold-ings* clothes   732 *toaze* tear   733 *cap-à-pie* from head to foot   739 *pheasant* i.e., as a bribe to the judge (the clown confuses the two kinds of courts)   749 *fantastical* odd   750 *picking on's teeth* (picking the teeth was an affectation of would-be gallants)

he shall know within this hour if I may come to the
speech of him.

AUTOLYCUS   Age, thou hast lost thy labor.   757

SHEPHERD   Why, sir?

AUTOLYCUS   The king is not at the palace. He is gone
aboard a new ship to purge melancholy and air himself,   760
for, if thou be'st capable of things serious, thou must
know the king is full of grief.

SHEPHERD   So 'tis said, sir – about his son, that should
have married a shepherd's daughter.

AUTOLYCUS   If that shepherd be not in handfast, let him   765
fly. The curses he shall have, the tortures he shall feel,
will break the back of man, the heart of monster.

CLOWN   Think you so, sir?

AUTOLYCUS   Not he alone shall suffer what wit can make
heavy and vengeance bitter; but those that are germane   770
to him, though removed fifty times, shall all come   771
under the hangman, which, though it be great pity, yet
it is necessary. An old sheep-whistling rogue, a ram tender, to offer to have his daughter come into grace!   774
Some say he shall be stoned, but that death is too soft
for him, say I. Draw our throne into a sheepcote! All
deaths are too few, the sharpest too easy.

CLOWN   Has the old man e'er a son, sir, do you hear, an't
like you, sir?

AUTOLYCUS   He has a son, who shall be flayed alive; then   780
'nointed over with honey, set on the head of a wasp's
nest; then stand till he be three quarters and a dram
dead; then recovered again with aqua vitae or some   783
other hot infusion. Then, raw as he is, and in the
hottest day prognostication proclaims, shall he be set   785
against a brick wall, the sun looking with a southward

---

757 *Age* old man   765 *handfast* custody   770 *germane* related   771 *removed . . . times* remotely   774 *grace* honor   783 *aqua vitae* brandy   785
prognostication forecast (forecasts for the coming year were published annu-
ally)

eye upon him, where he is to behold him with flies
blown to death. But what talk we of these traitorly ras-
cals, whose miseries are to be smiled at, their offenses
790   being so capital? Tell me, for you seem to be honest
791   plain men, what you have to the king. Being something
gently considered, I'll bring you where he is aboard,
tender your persons to his presence, whisper him in
your behalfs; and if it be in man besides the king to effect your suits, here is man shall do it.

796   CLOWN   He seems to be of great authority. Close with
him, give him gold; and though authority be a stub-
born bear, yet he is oft led by the nose with gold. Show
the inside of your purse to the outside of his hand, and
800   no more ado. Remember "stoned," and "flayed alive."

SHEPHERD   An't please you, sir, to undertake the business
for us, here is that gold I have. I'll make it as much
more and leave this young man in pawn till I bring it
you.

AUTOLYCUS   After I have done what I promised?

SHEPHERD   Ay, sir.

807   AUTOLYCUS   Well, give me the moiety. Are you a party in
this business?

809   CLOWN   In some sort, sir. But though my case be a piti-
810   ful one, I hope I shall not be flayed out of it.

AUTOLYCUS   O, that's the case of the shepherd's son.
Hang him, he'll be made an example.

CLOWN   Comfort, good comfort! We must to the king
and show our strange sights. He must know 'tis none of
815   your daughter nor my sister; we are gone else. Sir, I will
give you as much as this old man does when the business is performed, and remain, as he says, your pawn
till it be brought you.

791–92 *something . . . considered* given some consideration (i.e., bribe)   **796**
Close come to an agreement   **807** *moiety* half   **809** *case* (1) position in this
business, (2) skin   **815** *gone* undone

AUTOLYCUS I will trust you. Walk before toward the seaside. Go on the right hand. I will but look upon the 820
hedge and follow you.

CLOWN We are blest in this man, as I may say, even
blest.

SHEPHERD Let's before as he bids us. He was provided to
do us good. *[Exeunt Shepherd and Clown.]*

AUTOLYCUS If I had a mind to be honest, I see Fortune
would not suffer me; she drops booties in my mouth. I 827
am courted now with a double occasion, gold and a 828
means to do the prince my master good, which who
knows how that may turn back to my advancement? I 830
will bring these two moles, these blind ones, aboard 831
him. If he think it fit to shore them again and that the
complaint they have to the king concerns him nothing,
let him call me rogue for being so far officious, for I am
proof against that title and what shame else belongs to't.
To him will I present them; there may be matter in it.

Exit.

*

❧ **V.1** *Enter Leontes, Cleomenes, Dion, Paulina,*
Servants.

CLEOMENES
Sir, you have done enough, and have performed
A saintlike sorrow. No fault could you make
Which you have not redeemed – indeed, paid down
More penitence than done trespass. At the last,
Do as the heavens have done, forget your evil; 5
With them forgive yourself.

LEONTES Whilst I remember
Her and her virtues, I cannot forget

820–21 *look . . . hedge* urinate 827 *suffer* allow; *booties* rewards **828**
courted . . . with tempted now by **830** *turn back* revert **831–32** *aboard
him* to him aboard (the ship)
V.1 Leontes' palace 5 *evil* sin

8   My blemishes in them, and so still think of
The wrong I did myself, which was so much
10   That heirless it hath made my kingdom and
Destroyed the sweetest companion that e'er man
Bred his hopes out of. True?

PAULINA   Too true, my lord.
If one by one you wedded all the world,
Or from the all that are took something good
To make a perfect woman, she you killed
Would be unparalleled.

LEONTES   I think so. Killed?
She I killed? I did so, but thou strikest me
Sorely to say I did. It is as bitter
19   Upon thy tongue as in my thought. Now, good now,
20   Say so but seldom.

LEOMENES   Not at all, good lady.
You might have spoken a thousand things that would
22   Have done the time more benefit and graced
Your kindness better.

PAULINA   You are one of those
Would have him wed again.

DION   If you would not so,
You pity not the state nor the remembrance
Of his most sovereign name, consider little
27   What dangers, by his highness' fail of issue,
May drop upon his kingdom and devour
29   Incertain lookers on. What were more holy
30   Than to rejoice the former queen is well?
What holier than, for royalty's repair,
For present comfort and for future good,
To bless the bed of majesty again
With a sweet fellow to't?

PAULINA   There is none worthy,
35   Respecting her that's gone. Besides, the gods

---

8 *in* i.e., in relation to   19 *good now* i.e., I pray you   22 *graced* displayed
27 *fail of issue* lack of an heir   29 *Incertain* confused (as to an heir to the
throne)   35 *Respecting* compared to

Will have fulfilled their secret purposes;
For has not the divine Apollo said,
Is't not the tenor of his oracle,
That King Leontes shall not have an heir
Till his lost child be found? Which that it shall   *40*
Is all as monstrous to our human reason   *41*
As my Antigonus to break his grave
And come again to me, who, on my life,
Did perish with the infant. 'Tis your counsel
My lord should to the heavens be contrary,
Oppose against their wills.   *46*
     [To Leontes]   Care not for issue;
The crown will find an heir. Great Alexander   *47*
Left his to th' worthiest; so his successor
Was like to be the best.
LEONTES   Good Paulina,
Who hast the memory of Hermione,   *50*
I know, in honor, O that ever I
Had squared me to thy counsel! Then even now   *52*
I might have looked upon my queen's full eyes,
Have taken treasure from her lips –
PAULINA   And left them
More rich for what they yielded.
LEONTES   Thou speak'st truth.
No more such wives; therefore, no wife! One worse,   *56*
And better used, would make her sainted spirit
Again possess her corpse, and on this stage
(Where we offenders now) appear soul-vexed,   *59*
And begin, "Why to me?"   *60*
PAULINA   Had she such power,
She had just cause.
LEONTES   She had, and would incense me
To murder her I married.   *62*

---

41 *monstrous* incredible **46** *their* the gods' **47** *Great Alexander* (Alexander
advised that after his death the succession should be determined by merit,
not birth) **52** *squared me to* acted in accordance with **56** *No more* there are
no more **59** *now* now play our parts

PAULINA   I should so.
   Were I the ghost that walked, I'd bid you mark
   Her eye, and tell me for what dull part in't
   You chose her. Then I'd shriek, that even your ears
   Should rift to hear me, and the words that followed
   Should be "Remember mine."
LEONTES   Stars, stars,
   And all eyes else dead coals! Fear thou no wife;
   I'll have no wife, Paulina.
PAULINA   Will you swear
70   Never to marry but by my free leave?
LEONTES
   Never, Paulina, so be blest my spirit.
PAULINA
   Then, good my lords, bear witness to his oath.
CLEOMENES
73   You tempt him overmuch.
PAULINA   Unless another,
   As like Hermione as is her picture,
75   Affront his eye.
CLEOMENES   Good madam, I have done.
PAULINA
   Yet, if my lord will marry – if you will, sir,
   No remedy but you will – give me the office
   To choose you a queen. She shall not be so young
   As was your former, but she shall be such
80   As, walked your first queen's ghost, it should take joy
   To see her in your arms.
LEONTES   My true Paulina,
   We shall not marry till thou bid'st us.
PAULINA   That
83   Shall be when your first queen's again in breath.
   Never till then.
      Enter a Servant.

---

62 *should* should do   73 *tempt* urge   75 *Affront* confront   83 *in breath* alive

SERVANT
  One that gives out himself Prince Florizel,
  Son of Polixenes, with his princess – she
  The fairest I have yet beheld – desires access
  To your high presence.   88

LEONTES   What with him? He comes not
  Like to his father's greatness. His approach,   89
  So out of circumstance and sudden, tells us   90
  'Tis not a visitation framed, but forced   91
  By need and accident. What train?

SERVANT   But few,
  And those but mean.

LEONTES   His princess, say you, with him?

SERVANT
  Ay, the most peerless piece of earth, I think,
  That e'er the sun shone bright on.

PAULINA   O Hermione,
  As every present time doth boast itself
  Above a better gone, so must thy grave
  Give way to what's seen now. Sir, you yourself
  Have said and writ so, but your writing now
  Is colder than that theme. She had not been,   *100*
  Nor was not to be equaled – thus your verse
  Flowed with her beauty once. 'Tis shrewdly ebbed   *102*
  To say you have seen a better.

SERVANT   Pardon, madam.
  The one I have almost forgot – your pardon;
  The other, when she has obtained your eye,
  Will have your tongue too. This is a creature,
  Would she begin a sect, might quench the zeal
  Of all professors else, make proselytes   108
  Of who she but bid follow.

PAULINA   How? not women?

---

88 *What* who **89** *Like to* in a manner fitting; *approach* arrival **90** *out of circumstance* without formality **91** *framed* premeditated **102** *shrewdly* badly; *ebbed* declined **108** *professors else* those who profess other faiths

SERVANT

110   Women will love her that she is a woman
More worth than any man; men, that she is
The rarest of all women.

LEONTES   Go, Cleomenes.
Yourself, assisted with your honored friends,
Bring them to our embracement.

                     Exit [Cleomenes with others].
                     Still, 'tis strange

115   He thus should steal upon us.

PAULINA   Had our prince,
Jewel of children, seen this hour, he had paired
Well with this lord. There was not full a month
Between their births.

LEONTES
Prithee, no more; cease. Thou know'st

120   He dies to me again when talked of. Sure,
When I shall see this gentleman, thy speeches
Will bring me to consider that which may

123   Unfurnish me of reason. They are come.

    Enter Florizel, Perdita, Cleomenes, and others.
Your mother was most true to wedlock, prince,
For she did print your royal father off,
Conceiving you. Were I but twenty-one,
Your father's image is so hit in you,
His very air, that I should call you brother,
As I did him, and speak of something wildly

130   By us performed before. Most dearly welcome!
And your fair princess – goddess! O, alas!
I lost a couple that 'twixt heaven and earth
Might thus have stood begetting wonder as
You, gracious couple, do. And then I lost –
All mine own folly – the society,
Amity too, of your brave father, whom,

137   Though bearing misery, I desire my life

---

115 *steal . . . us* i.e., come unannounced **123** *Unfurnish* deprive **137–38**
I . . . him I would give my life to see him one more time

   Once more to look on him.

FLORIZEL   By his command
   Have I here touched Sicilia, and from him
   Give you all greetings that a king, at friend,   140
   Can send his brother; and, but infirmity
   Which waits upon worn times hath something seized   142
   His wished ability, he had himself
   The lands and waters 'twixt your throne and his
   Measured to look upon you, whom he loves –   145
   He bade me say so – more than all the scepters
   And those that bear them living.

LEONTES   O my brother,
   Good gentleman, the wrongs I have done thee stir
   Afresh within me, and these thy offices,   149
   So rarely kind, are as interpreters   150
   Of my behindhand slackness. Welcome hither,
   As is the spring to th' earth. And hath he too
   Exposed this paragon to th' fearful usage,
   At least ungentle, of the dreadful Neptune,
   To greet a man not worth her pains, much less
   Th' adventure of her person?   156

FLORIZEL   Good my lord,
   She came from Libya.

LEONTES   Where the warlike Smalus,
   That noble honored lord, is feared and loved?

FLORIZEL
   Most royal sir, from thence, from him, whose daughter
   His tears proclaimed his, parting with her. Thence,   *160*
   A prosperous south wind friendly, we have crossed,
   To execute the charge my father gave me
   For visiting your highness. My best train
   I have from your Sicilian shores dismissed,
   Who for Bohemia bend, to signify

---

140 *at friend* in friendship **142** *waits . . . times* accompanies old age; *something seized* somewhat taken away **145** *Measured* journeyed over **149** *offices* courtesies **150–51** *are . . . slackness* emphasize my tardy, inadequate action **156** *adventure* risk

Not only my success in Libya, sir,
But my arrival and my wife's in safety
Here where we are.

LEONTES   The blessèd gods
Purge all infection from our air whilst you
170 Do climate here! You have a holy father,
171 A graceful gentleman, against whose person,
So sacred as it is, I have done sin,
For which the heavens, taking angry note,
Have left me issueless; and your father's blest,
As he from heaven merits it, with you,
Worthy his goodness. What might I have been,
Might I a son and daughter now have looked on,
Such goodly things as you?

        Enter a Lord.

LORD   Most noble sir,
179 That which I shall report will bear no credit,
180 Were not the proof so nigh. Please you, great sir,
Bohemia greets you from himself by me,
182 Desires you to attach his son, who has –
His dignity and duty both cast off –
Fled from his father, from his hopes, and with
A shepherd's daughter.

LEONTES   Where's Bohemia? Speak.

LORD
Here in your city. I now came from him.
187 I speak amazedly, and it becomes
My marvel and my message. To your court
189 Whiles he was hastening – in the chase, it seems,
190 Of this fair couple – meets he on the way
The father of this seeming lady and
Her brother, having both their country quitted
With this young prince.

---

170 *climate* dwell   171 *graceful* gracious   179 *bear no credit* not be believed
182 *attach* arrest   187 *amazedly* confusedly   187–88 *it . . . marvel* my confused speech suits (results from) my wonder   189 *chase* pursuit

FLORIZEL   Camillo has betrayed me,
　Whose honor and whose honesty till now
　Endured all weathers.
LORD   Lay't so to his charge.
　He's with the king your father.
LEONTES   Who? Camillo?
LORD
　Camillo, sir. I spake with him, who now
　Has these poor men in question. Never saw I   198
　Wretches so quake. They kneel, they kiss the earth,
　Forswear themselves as often as they speak.   *200*
　Bohemia stops his ears, and threatens them
　With divers deaths in death.   *202*
PERDITA   O my poor father!
　The heaven sets spies upon us, will not have
　Our contract celebrated.
LEONTES   You are married?
FLORIZEL
　We are not, sir, nor are we like to be.
　The stars, I see, will kiss the valleys first;
　The odds for high and low's alike.   207
LEONTES   My lord,
　Is this the daughter of a king?
FLORIZEL   She is
　When once she is my wife.
LEONTES
　That "once," I see by your good father's speed,   *210*
　Will come on very slowly. I am sorry,
　Most sorry, you have broken from his liking
　Where you were tied in duty, and as sorry
　Your choice is not so rich in worth as beauty,   214
　That you might well enjoy her.
FLORIZEL   Dear, look up.
　Though Fortune, visible an enemy,   216

---

198 *these . . . men* (i.e., the shepherd and the clown)　**202** *deaths in death* tortures　**207** *odds . . . alike* high and low are alike subject to misfortune　**214** *worth* high birth　**216** *visible* clearly

Should chase us with my father, power no jot
Hath she to change our loves. Beseech you, sir,
219 Remember since you owed no more to time
220 Than I do now. With thought of such affections,
Step forth mine advocate. At your request
My father will grant precious things as trifles.

LEONTES
Would he do so, I'd beg your precious mistress,
Which he counts but a trifle.

PAULINA   Sir, my liege,
Your eye hath too much youth in't. Not a month
'Fore your queen died, she was more worth such gazes
Than what you look on now.

LEONTES   I thought of her
Even in these looks I made. *[To Florizel]* But your peti-
tion
Is yet unanswered. I will to your father.
230 Your honor not o'erthrown by your desires,
I am friend to them and you. Upon which errand
I now go toward him; therefore follow me
233 And mark what way I make. Come, good my lord.
                                       Exeunt.

*

∞ **V.2** *Enter Autolycus and a Gentleman.*

AUTOLYCUS   Beseech you, sir, were you present at this relation?

FIRST GENTLEMAN   I was by at the opening of the fardel,
heard the old shepherd deliver the manner how he
found it; whereupon, after a little amazedness, we were
all commanded out of the chamber. Only this

219–20 *since . . . now* when you were my age   **230** *Your . . . desires* if your
desires have not led you to do what is dishonorable (i.e., to have sex with
Perdita)   **233** *way* progress
V.2 In or near Leontes' palace

methought I heard the shepherd say, he found the
child.

AUTOLYCUS   I would most gladly know the issue of it.   9

FIRST GENTLEMAN   I make a broken delivery of the busi-   10
ness; but the changes I perceived in the king and
Camillo were very notes of admiration. They seemed   12
almost, with staring on one another, to tear the cases of
their eyes. There was speech in their dumbness, language in their very gesture. They looked as they had
heard of a world ransomed, or one destroyed. A notable
passion of wonder appeared in them. But the wisest be-   17
holder, that knew no more but seeing, could not say if   18
the importance were joy or sorrow; but in the extremity   19
of the one, it must needs be.   20

Enter another Gentleman.

Here comes a gentleman that haply knows more. The   21
news, Rogero?

SECOND GENTLEMAN   Nothing but bonfires. The oracle   23
is fulfilled; the king's daughter is found. Such a deal of
wonder is broken out within this hour that ballad-
makers cannot be able to express it.

Enter another Gentleman.

Here comes the Lady Paulina's steward; he can deliver   27
you more. How goes it now, sir? This news which is
called true is so like an old tale that the verity of it is in
strong suspicion. Has the king found his heir?   30

THIRD GENTLEMAN   Most true, if ever truth were pregnant   31
by circumstance. That which you hear you'll swear you
see, there is such unity in the proofs. The mantle of   33
Queen Hermione's, her jewel about the neck of it, the
letters of Antigonus found with it, which they know to
be his character, the majesty of the creature in resem-   36

---

9 *issue* outcome   10 *make . . . delivery* give a fragmentary account   12 *admiration* wonder   17 *passion* emotion   18 *seeing* what he saw   19 *importance* import   21 *haply* perhaps   23 *bonfires* (common Elizabethan way to
mark significant public occasions)   27 *deliver* tell   31–32 *pregnant by circumstance* obvious from the evidence   33 *unity* agreement   36 *character*
handwriting

37   blance of the mother, the affection of nobleness which
      nature shows above her breeding, and many other evi-
      dences proclaim her with all certainty to be the king's
40   daughter. Did you see the meeting of the two kings?
      SECOND GENTLEMAN   No.
      THIRD GENTLEMAN   Then have you lost a sight which
      was to be seen, cannot be spoken of. There might you
      have beheld one joy crown another, so and in such
      manner that it seemed sorrow wept to take leave of
      them, for their joy waded in tears. There was casting up
47   of eyes, holding up of hands, with countenance of such
      distraction that they were to be known by garment, not
      by favor. Our king, being ready to leap out of himself
50   for joy of his found daughter, as if that joy were now
      become a loss, cries, "O, thy mother, thy mother!" then
      asks Bohemia forgiveness; then embraces his son-in-
53   law; then again worries he his daughter with clipping
      her; now he thanks the old shepherd, which stands by
55   like a weather-bitten conduit of many kings' reigns. I
      never heard of such another encounter, which lames re-
57   port to follow it and undoes description to do it.
      SECOND   GENTLEMAN   What, pray you, became of
      Antigonus, that carried hence the child?
60   THIRD GENTLEMAN   Like an old tale still, which will have
61   matter to rehearse, though credit be asleep and not an
62   ear open. He was torn to pieces with a bear. This
63   avouches the shepherd's son, who has not only his in-
      nocence, which seems much, to justify him, but a hand-
      kerchief and rings of his that Paulina knows.
      FIRST GENTLEMAN   What became of his bark and his fol-
      lowers?

---

37 *affection of* natural tendency toward   47–49 *with . . . favor* with their
faces so altered by emotion that they must be distinguished by their clothes
rather than their features   53 *clipping* embracing   55 *conduit* structure from
which flows water (here tears)   57 *undoes . . . it* renders description incapable of describing   61 *matter to rehearse* something to relate; *credit* belief
62 *with* by   63–64 *innocence* simplicity

THIRD GENTLEMAN   Wrecked the same instant of their
master's death and in the view of the shepherd; so that
all the instruments which aided to expose the child   *70*
were even then lost when it was found. But O, the
noble combat that 'twixt joy and sorrow was fought in
Paulina! She had one eye declined for the loss of her   *73*
husband, another elevated that the oracle was fulfilled.
She lifted the princess from the earth, and so locks her
in embracing as if she would pin her to her heart that
she might no more be in danger of losing.

FIRST GENTLEMAN   The dignity of this act was worth the
audience of kings and princes, for by such was it acted.

THIRD GENTLEMAN   One of the prettiest touches of all,   *80*
and that which angled for mine eyes, caught the water   *81*
though not the fish, was when, at the relation of the
queen's death, with the manner how she came to't
bravely confessed and lamented by the king, how
attentiveness wounded his daughter, till, from one sign   *85*
of dolor to another, she did, with an "Alas," I would
fain say, bleed tears, for I am sure my heart wept blood.
Who was most marble there changed color; some
swooned, all sorrowed. If all the world could have
seen't, the woe had been universal.   *90*

FIRST GENTLEMAN   Are they returned to the court?

THIRD GENTLEMAN   No. The princess, hearing of her
mother's statue, which is in the keeping of Paulina – a
piece many years in doing and now newly performed   *94*
by that rare Italian master, Giulio Romano, who, had   *95*
he himself eternity and could put breath into his work,
would beguile Nature of her custom, so perfectly he is   *97*
her ape. He so near to Hermione hath done Hermione   *98*
that they say one would speak to her and stand in hope

---

73 *declined* cast down in sorrow   **81** *the water* my tears   **85** *attentiveness* listening   **94** *performed* finished   **95** *Romano* (an Italian painter and sculptor who died in 1546)   **97** *beguile . . . custom* rob Nature of her business (i.e., creating living people)   **98** *her ape* Nature's imitator

100   of answer. Thither with all greediness of affection are
they gone, and there they intend to sup.

SECOND GENTLEMAN   I thought she had some great matter there in hand, for she hath privately twice or thrice
a day, ever since the death of Hermione, visited that removed house. Shall we thither and with our company
106   piece the rejoicing?

FIRST GENTLEMAN   Who would be thence that has the
benefit of access? Every wink of an eye some new grace
109   will be born. Our absence makes us unthrifty to our
110   knowledge. Let's along.   *Exeunt [Gentlemen].*

111 AUTOLYCUS   Now, had I not the dash of my former life in
112   me, would preferment drop on my head. I brought the
113   old man and his son aboard the prince, told him I
heard them talk of a fardel and I know not what. But
he at that time, overfond of the shepherd's daughter –
so he then took her to be – who began to be much sea-
sick, and himself little better, extremity of weather con-
tinuing, this mystery remained undiscovered. But 'tis
all one to me; for had I been the finder out of this se-
120   cret, it would not have relished among my other dis-
credits.

    Enter Shepherd and Clown.

Here come those I have done good to against my will,
and already appearing in the blossoms of their fortune.

SHEPHERD   Come, boy. I am past more children, but thy
sons and daughters will be all gentlemen born.

126 CLOWN   You are well met, sir. You denied to fight with
me this other day, because I was no gentleman born.
See you these clothes? Say you see them not and think
129   me still no gentleman born. You were best say these
130   robes are not gentlemen born. Give me the lie, do, and
try whether I am not now a gentleman born.

---

106 *piece* add to   **109** *unthrifty to* failing to add to   **111** *dash* taint   **112**
preferment advancement, promotion   **113** *the prince* the prince's ship   **120**
relished (1) fitted in, (2) seemed as pleasing   **126** *denied* refused   **129**
were . . . say i.e., might as well say   **130** *Give . . . lie* (say I'm not a gentleman
again, which is now a lie, so that I can challenge you to a duel)

AUTOLYCUS   I know you are now, sir, a gentleman born.

CLOWN   Ay, and have been so any time these four hours.

SHEPHERD   And so have I, boy.

CLOWN   So you have. But I was a gentleman born before
my father, for the king's son took me by the hand and
called me brother; and then the two kings called my father brother; and then the prince my brother and the
princess my sister called my father father; and so we
wept, and there was the first gentleman-like tears that   *140*
ever we shed.

SHEPHERD   We may live, son, to shed many more.

CLOWN   Ay, or else 'twere hard luck, being in so pre-   *143*
posterous estate as we are.

AUTOLYCUS   I humbly beseech you, sir, to pardon me all
the faults I have committed to your worship and to give
me your good report to the prince my master.

SHEPHERD   Prithee, son, do, for we must be gentle now
we are gentlemen.

CLOWN   Thou wilt amend thy life?   *150*

AUTOLYCUS   Ay, an it like your good worship.   *151*

CLOWN   Give me thy hand. I will swear to the prince
thou art as honest a true fellow as any is in Bohemia.

SHEPHERD   You may say it, but not swear it.

CLOWN   Not swear it, now I am a gentleman? Let boors   *155*
and franklins say it, I'll swear it.   *156*

SHEPHERD   How if it be false, son?

CLOWN   If it be ne'er so false, a true gentleman may
swear it in the behalf of his friend. And I'll swear to the
prince thou art a tall fellow of thy hands and that thou   *160*
wilt not be drunk; but I know thou art no tall fellow of
thy hands and that thou wilt be drunk. But I'll swear it,
and I would thou wouldst be a tall fellow of thy hands.

AUTOLYCUS   I will prove so, sir, to my power.

143–44 *preposterous* (the clown seems to intend "prosperous," but since the word "preposterous" brings together contraries [the before and the after], it also signals the inversion by which the shepherds have become *gentlemen born*)   151 *an it like* if it please   155 *boors* peasants   156 *franklins* small landowners, farmers   160 *tall . . . hands* bold fellow, quick to act

CLOWN Ay, by any means prove a tall fellow. If I do not
wonder how thou darest venture to be drunk, not
being a tall fellow, trust me not. Hark! The kings and
the princes, our kindred, are going to see the queen's
169 picture. Come, follow us. We'll be thy good masters.
Exeunt.

*

❧ **V.3** *Enter Leontes, Polixenes, Florizel, Perdita,*
Camillo, Paulina, Lords, etc.

LEONTES
O grave and good Paulina, the great comfort
That I have had of thee!
PAULINA   What, sovereign sir,
I did not well, I meant well. All my services
4   You have paid home. But that you have vouchsafed,
5   With your crowned brother and these your contracted
Heirs of your kingdoms, my poor house to visit,
7   It is a surplus of your grace which never
8   My life may last to answer.
LEONTES   O Paulina,
9   We honor you with trouble. But we came
10 To see the statue of our queen. Your gallery
Have we passed through, not without much content
12 In many singularities; but we saw not
That which my daughter came to look upon,
The statue of her mother.
PAULINA   .   As she lived peerless,
So her dead likeness, I do well believe,
Excels whatever yet you looked upon
Or hand of man hath done. Therefore I keep it

---

169 *picture* likeness; *good masters* benefactors
V.3 Within Paulina's house **4** *paid home* rewarded handsomely; *vouch-*
safed sworn **5** *contracted* engaged **7** *surplus . . . grace* additional show of
your kindness **8** *answer* repay in kind **9** *with trouble* only by making you
go to trouble **10** *gallery* a hall in which works of art are displayed **12** *sin-*
gularities rarities

Lonely, apart. But here it is. Prepare
To see the life as lively mocked as ever   19
Still sleep mocked death. Behold, and say 'tis well.   20
   [Paulina reveals] Hermione [standing] like a statue.
I like your silence; it the more shows off
Your wonder. But yet speak; first, you, my liege.
Comes it not something near?

LEONTES   Her natural posture!
Chide me, dear stone, that I may say indeed
Thou art Hermione; or rather, thou art she
In thy not chiding, for she was as tender
As infancy and grace. But yet, Paulina,
Hermione was not so much wrinkled, nothing
So aged as this seems.

POLIXENES   O, not by much.

PAULINA
So much the more our carver's excellence,   30
Which lets go by some sixteen years and makes her   31
As she lived now.

LEONTES   As now she might have done,
So much to my good comfort, as it is
Now piercing to my soul. O, thus she stood,
Even with such life of majesty – warm life,
As now it coldly stands – when first I wooed her!
I am ashamed. Does not the stone rebuke me
For being more stone than it? O royal piece,   38
There's magic in thy majesty, which has
My evils conjured to remembrance and   40
From thy admiring daughter took the spirits,   41
Standing like stone with thee.

PERDITA   And give me leave,
And do not say 'tis superstition, that   43

---

19 *lively mocked* vividly imitated   31 *lets go by* i.e., indicates the passage of
38 *piece* (1) person, (2) statue   40 *conjured* summoned   41 *admiring* wondering   43 *superstition* (an anachronistic allusion to Protestant objections to
idolatry, especially to kneeling before and worshiping images of the Virgin
Mary)

I kneel and then implore her blessing. Lady,
Dear queen, that ended when I but began,
Give me that hand of yours to kiss.

PAULINA   O, patience!
47   The statue is but newly fixed, the color's
      Not dry.

CAMILLO
      My lord, your sorrow was too sore laid on,
50   Which sixteen winters cannot blow away,
      So many summers dry. Scarce any joy
      Did ever so long live; no sorrow
      But killed itself much sooner.

POLIXENES   Dear my brother,
      Let him that was the cause of this have power
      To take off so much grief from you as he
56   Will piece up in himself.

PAULINA   Indeed, my lord,
      If I had thought the sight of my poor image
58   Would thus have wrought you – for the stone is mine –
      I'd not have showed it.

LEONTES   Do not draw the curtain.

PAULINA
60   No longer shall you gaze on't, lest your fancy
      May think anon it moves.

LEONTES   Let be, let be.
      Would I were dead, but that, methinks, already –
      What was he that did make it? See, my lord,
      Would you not deem it breathed? and that those veins
      Did verily bear blood?

POLIXENES   Masterly done.
      The very life seems warm upon her lip.

LEONTES
67   The fixture of her eye has motion in't,
68   As we are mocked with art.

_____

47 *fixed* painted   56 *piece up* make up   58 *wrought you* gotten you so
worked up   60 *fancy* imagination   67 *The fixture . . . in't* the way the eye is
set makes it seem to move   68 *As* so that

PAULINA   I'll draw the curtain.
  My lord's almost so far transported that
  He'll think anon it lives.   70
LEONTES   O sweet Paulina,
  Make me to think so twenty years together!
  No settled senses of the world can match   72
  The pleasure of that madness. Let't alone.
PAULINA
  I am sorry, sir, I have thus far stirred you; but
  I could afflict you farther.
LEONTES   Do, Paulina,
  For this affliction has a taste as sweet
  As any cordial comfort. Still methinks
  There is an air comes from her. What fine chisel
  Could ever yet cut breath? Let no man mock me,
  For I will kiss her.   80
PAULINA   Good my lord, forbear.
  The ruddiness upon her lip is wet;
  You'll mar it if you kiss it, stain your own
  With oily painting. Shall I draw the curtain?
LEONTES
  No, not these twenty years.
PERDITA   So long could I
  Stand by, a looker on.
PAULINA   Either forbear,
  Quit presently the chapel, or resolve you   86
  For more amazement. If you can behold it,
  I'll make the statue move indeed, descend
  And take you by the hand. But then you'll think –
  Which I protest against – I am assisted   90
  By wicked powers.
LEONTES   What you can make her do,
  I am content to look on; what to speak,
  I am content to hear; for 'tis as easy
  To make her speak as move.

---

72 *settled* calm, sane   86 *presently* at once; *resolve* prepare

PAULINA   It is required
You do awake your faith. Then all stand still;
96   Or those that think it is unlawful business
I am about, let them depart.
LEONTES   Proceed.
No foot shall stir.
PAULINA   Music! Awake her, strike!
    [Music.]
'Tis time; descend; be stone no more; approach;
100   Strike all that look upon with marvel. Come,
I'll fill your grave up. Stir, nay, come away;
102   Bequeath to death your numbness, for from him
Dear life redeems you. You perceive she stirs.
    [Hermione comes down.]
Start not; her actions shall be holy as
You hear my spell is lawful. Do not shun her
Until you see her die again, for then
107   You kill her double. Nay, present your hand.
When she was young you wooed her; now in age
Is she become the suitor?
LEONTES   O, she's warm!
110   If this be magic, let it be an art
Lawful as eating.
POLIXENES   She embraces him.
CAMILLO
She hangs about his neck.
113   If she pertain to life, let her speak too.
POLIXENES
Ay, and make it manifest where she has lived,
Or how stolen from the dead.
PAULINA   That she is living,
Were it but told you, should be hooted at
Like an old tale; but it appears she lives,
Though yet she speak not. Mark a little while.

---

96 *unlawful* unnatural, occult   102 *him* i.e., death   107 *double* a second
time   113 *pertain to life* belongs with the living

Please you to interpose, fair madam. Kneel   119
And pray your mother's blessing. Turn, good lady;   *120*
Our Perdita is found.
HERMIONE   You gods, look down,
And from your sacred vials pour your graces   122
Upon my daughter's head! Tell me, mine own,
Where hast thou been preserved? where lived? how
    found
Thy father's court? For thou shalt hear that I,
Knowing by Paulina that the oracle
Gave hope thou wast in being, have preserved
Myself to see the issue.
PAULINA   There's time enough for that,
Lest they desire upon this push to trouble   129
Your joys with like relation. Go together,   130
You precious winners all; your exultation   131
Partake to every one. I, an old turtle,   132
Will wing me to some withered bough and there
My mate, that's never to be found again,
Lament till I am lost.
LEONTES   O, peace, Paulina!
Thou shouldst a husband take by my consent,
As I by thine a wife. This is a match,
And made between's by vows. Thou hast found mine;
But how, is to be questioned, for I saw her,
As I thought, dead, and have in vain said many   *140*
A prayer upon her grave. I'll not seek far –
For him, I partly know his mind – to find thee
An honorable husband. Come, Camillo,
And take her by the hand, whose worth and honesty
Is richly noted and here justified   145
By us, a pair of kings. Let's from this place.

---

119 *interpose* come between (Hermione and Leontes)   122 *graces* blessings
129 *upon this push* at this point   130 *like relation* similar account   131–32
your exultation . . . to share your joy with   132 *turtle* turtledove (a symbol of
faithful love and of sadness)   145 *justified* vouched for

What! look upon my brother. Both your pardons,
148   That e'er I put between your holy looks
     My ill suspicion. This your son-in-law
150   And son unto the king, whom heavens directing,
     Is trothplight to your daughter. Good Paulina,
     Lead us from hence, where we may leisurely
     Each one demand and answer to his part
     Performed in this wide gap of time since first
155   We were dissevered. Hastily lead away.   *Exeunt.*

---

148 *holy* chaste   **155** *dissevered* separated